PERGAMON INTERNATIONAL LIBRARY
of Science, Technology, Engineering and Social Studies

*The 1000-volume original paperback library in aid of education,
industrial training and the enjoyment of leisure*

Publisher: Robert Maxwell, M.C.

Applied Productivity
Analysis for Industry

OMEGA MANAGEMENT SCIENCE SERIES
Editor: Professor S. Eilon

Some Other Titles in this Series

GOLD, BELA	Technological Change: Economics, Management and Environment
KING, J. R.	Production Planning and Control

Other Titles of Interest

DUBRIN, A. J.	The Practice of Managerial Psychology
DUBRIN, A. J.	Fundamentals of Organizational Behaviour
TOWNSEND, H.	Scale, Innovation, Merger and Monopoly
HUSSEY, D. E.	Introducing Corporate Planning
HUSSEY, D. E.	Corporate Planning: Theory and Practice
IBRAHIM, I. B., SEO, K. K. and VLACHEOS, P. G.	Readings in Managerial Economics
LETHBRIDGE, DAVID G.	Government and Industry Relationships

The terms of our inspection copy service apply to all the above books. A complete catalogue of all books in the Pergamon International Library is available on request.

Applied Productivity Analysis for Industry

SAMUEL EILON
BELA GOLD
and
JUDITH SOESAN

PERGAMON PRESS

Oxford · New York · Toronto
Paris · Sydney · Braunschweig

U. K.	Pergamon Press Ltd., Headington Hill Hall, Oxford OX3 0BW, England
U. S. A.	Pergamon Press Inc., Maxwell House, Fairview Park, Elmsford, New York 10523, U.S.A.
C A N A D A	Pergamon of Canada, Ltd., 207 Queen's Quay West, Toronto 1, Canada
A U S T R A L I A	Pergamon Press (Aust.) Pty. Ltd., 19a Boundary Street, Rushcutters Bay, N.S.W. 2011, Australia
F R A N C E	Pergamon Press SARL, 24 rue des Ecoles, 75240 Paris, Cedex 05, France
WEST GERMANY	Pergamon Press GMbH, D-3300 Braunschweig, Burgplatz 1, West Germany

First edition 1976

Library of Congress Cataloging in Publication Data

Eilon, Samuel.
Applied productivity analysis for industry.

(Omega management science series) (Pergamon international library of science, technology, engineering, and social studies)
Includes index.
1. Industrial productivity. 2. Efficiency, Industrial. I. Gold, Bela, joint author.
II. Soesan, Judith, joint author. III. Title.
T58.8.E34 1976   658.5'1   75-38936
ISBN 0-08-020507-0
ISBN 0-08-020506-2 pbk.

Printed in Great Britain by A. Wheaton & Co. Exeter

Contents

Preface

The major purposes of this volume are:

(a) To transform the generally understood but essentially amorphous concept of *productivity* into one which is defined sharply enough to be used for actual industrial operations.

(b) To demonstrate that a set of specific productivity measures suggested in this volume can be applied to successively larger units of a firm, from production or cost centres to departments, as well as to the entire firm.

(c) To provide the appropriate levels of the managerial hierarchy with a practical analytical framework for the evaluation of past operations and for the planning of future activities, including the assessment of various alternative possibilities.

The importance of such a methodology lies in the urgent need for effective tools for measuring productivity changes, not only at the national and industry levels—where such studies have become commonplace—but also at the plant level, where decisions must be made about costly inputs to manufacturing processes, about investment in equipment, and about effecting technological change and adjustments in product-mix; this is where, as a result of such efforts, competitive advantages and disadvantages are generated. Because of the different timing and effects of changes in technology as compared with the impacts of adjustments in such economic factors as output, input factor prices and product prices, it is important to segregate their respective influences on the productivity relationships entering into managerial evaluations of performance. And because of the joint contributions of purchased supplies, capital facilities and labour to the effectiveness of industrial operations—as well as of their joint sharing of resulting revenues—it is of critical importance to develop increasingly persuasive measures of their respective contributions to the jointly determined outcomes.

This book is divided into three parts: the first is devoted to a discussion of the current concept of productivity and its definitions, and to a literature survey of various prevailing approaches to the problem (Chapter 1). It then proceeds to propose a framework for productivity analysis and an array of management-control ratios (Chapter 2) and also to indicate how problems of measurement can be overcome in practical situations (Chapter 3).

The second part describes five case studies to illustrate how the proposed methodology can be applied in various situations involving different levels of complexity and aggregation: the first case study is concerned with an example from the chemical industry, where the production process involves a relatively small number of inputs and outputs (Chapter 4). Three case studies are then described for the analysis of three departments in a steel plant: the first relying on many inputs from the outside, the second having its major inputs and outputs from and to other departments, the third producing numerous products. These case studies show how the analysis can be adapted to handle the various circumstances encountered in these departments and how it can be used to assess the impact of technological change and increasing labour costs (Chapter 5). The fifth case study covers the whole steel plant and demonstrates the use of managerial-control ratios for the evaluation of performance (Chapter 6).

The third part is devoted to discussion and conclusions: first, various problems encountered during the case studies in measurement and analysis are reviewed and suggestions are made as to how they can be overcome (Chapter 7); secondly, the use of the model for planning purposes is discussed, through the means of sensitivity tables, deterministic appraisals and risk simulation (Chapter 8). The concluding chapter (Chapter 9) suggests that the methodology employed in this book can be applied to various industries.

This book describes the collaborative research project in the measurement of productivity conducted in the Department of Management Science, Imperial College, London, during the period 1970-4. The effort at Imperial College has been directed towards appraising the applicability of various approaches which have been proposed to measure productivity at the level of the firm and of its component parts, and then testing through empirical work the applicability of a productivity model which has been developed to help managers in the analysis of industrial operations.

One of the authors, Professor Gold of Case Western Reserve University in Cleveland, Ohio, has been concerned with productivity studies in the United States for many years and the work of his Research Program in Industrial Economics has covered a variety of industries, ranging from steel to agriculture, at various levels of aggregation. The collaborative work across the Atlantic was helped through several visits to Cleveland by Professor Eilon, who was a Professorial Research Fellow at Case Western Reserve University in its Research Program in Industrial Economics, and by visits to London by Professor Gold, who also spent a sabbatical year in 1973 at Imperial College and initiated the field work of the steel-plant study. Miss Soesan held a Fellowship and later a Research Assistantship in the Department of Management Science, Imperial College, in 1970-4.

The authors wish to record their sincere thanks to the British Oxygen Co. Ltd. and the Chairman Leslie Smith for setting up a Fellowship at Imperial College and for providing facilities for case study work in various plants and particularly to David Pitts, the then Chief Executive of the Gases Division, and George Prosper, the Branch Manager at Newport, for their continuous support; to the British Steel Corporation—to B. Darnell, R. Scholey and J. R. C. Boys, and particularly to Peter Allen, Director in Charge of the Port Talbot Works, and Terry Price of the Cost Department—for help in the massive data-collection exercise; and to the Social Science Research Council in the U.K. for financial support during 1972-4. Empirical research in the field of Industrial Economics is a time-consuming business; it is also fraught with numerous difficulties, which could only be overcome with the collaboration of many managers at various levels of the hierarchical structure of the companies involved in the case studies. For their help, advice and patience, the authors are most grateful.

SAMUEL EILON
BELA GOLD
JUDITH SOESAN

PART ONE

Definitions, Concepts and Measures

CHAPTER 1

Definitions and Prevailing Approaches

SAMUEL EILON and JUDITH SOESAN

Introduction

The welfare of individual enterprises, and even of entire national economies, is widely regarded as dependent on their comparative productivity. Changes in productivity levels are being increasingly recognized as a major influence on a wide range of social and economic considerations, such as rapid growth, higher standards of living, improvements in the balance of payments, inflation control and leisure. The very importance of these objectives, however, emphasizes the seriousness of continued widespread misunderstanding of the nature and effects of productivity adjustments.

Productivity is generally interpreted as "efficiency in industrial production"[1] to be measured by some relationship of outputs to inputs. As summarized by the *Encyclopaedia Britannica*:[2] "Productivity in economics is the ratio of what is produced to what is required to produce it. Usually this ratio is in the form of an average, expressing the total output of some category of goods divided by the total input of, say, labour or raw materials. In principle, any input can be used in the denominator of the productivity ratio. Thus, one can speak of the productivity of land, labour, capital, or sub-categories of any of these factors of production." The author of the article proceeds to state that "Labour is by far the commonest of the factors used in measuring productivity. One reason for this is, of course, that labour inputs are measured more easily than certain other factors, such as capital", particularly when the measurement of labour is based on a head-count or on statistics of hours worked, ignoring differences in skill and rates of pay.

Another reason for labour productivity being so prominent is that productivity adjustments have become central in many wage negotiations, with or without the support of government pressures to link wage settlements to productivity. This reflects the desire of labour unions to ensure that an improvement in performance of an industrial enterprise is coupled with improved wages and working conditions, and it also reflects the parallel concern of management to achieve improvements in performance in order to help offset the costs of higher payments to labour. Together, these convergent concerns raise several critical questions:

1. Assuming that improvement in overall performance can be measured, how closely can we determine the relative contribution of labour and of other factors to such

---

[1] *The Oxford Illustrated Dictionary.*
[2] 1974 edition.

3

improvement?

2. Having determined the relative contributions of the major input factors, what adjustments in their respective rewards would be appropriate?
3. When improvements in labour's contributions are not accompanied by improvements in the performance of the enterprise as a whole, should labour's compensation be increased none the less?
4. When improvements in the performance of the enterprise are not due to labour contributions, should labour nevertheless have a share in the benefits to the enterprise, and if so how much?
5. Should a higher productivity-linked compensation become operative only after increases in productivity materialize, or should it be paid on the basis of future expected performance?

These questions reflect the main themes associated with productivity-linked wage agreements and they continue to dominate many texts devoted to the study of productivity. I. G. Smith, for example, is solely concerned with "the process of productivity bargaining" and seeks "to prove that this process does represent a practical method for raising *total* productivity" [27, p. 3]. He then records the number of agreements in the U.K. (covered in a survey published in 1969) which involved the removal of restrictive practices and the introduction of technological change, such as speeding up or replacing machinery, abolition of tea breaks, increased flexibility between crafts, reduction in manning, etc. [27, p. 13]. He points out the commonly accepted notion of a measurement of productivity based on a reduction of costs per unit of output or on a reduction in overtime hours, but he questions whether such measures reflect growth in output and he repeatedly states that labour productivity is only a partial definition of productivity, echoing similar statements from other writers (see, for example, [11]). Other examples of notable texts devoted to productivity bargaining are those by E. Owen Smith, who concentrates on British Steel as a case study [26], and by Flanders who discusses a well-known case in the oil industry [10].

The theme of productivity agreements in the 1960s in the U.K. was largely centred on providing "changes in working practices for the purpose of improving the utilization of both capital and labour, in return for improvements in pay" [16, 19]. The productivity criterion was first defined in the 1965 Government White Paper on Prices and Incomes (in the U.K.), and then repeated in the 1967 White Paper, allowing pay increases above the norm "where the employees concerned, for example by accepting more exacting work or a major change in working practices, make a direct contribution towards increasing productivity in the particular firm or industry".

These sentiments were further expanded in 1967 by the National Board for Prices and Incomes in the U.K. [19, p. 45]:

"we would, for the guidance of managements, unions, and the Ministry of Labour, rewrite the seven guidelines as follows:

(i) It should be shown that workers are making a direct contribution towards increasing productivity by accepting more exacting work or a major change in working practices.

(ii) Forecasts of increased productivity should be derived by the application of proper work-standards.

(iii) An accurate calculation of the gains and the costs should normally show that

4

the total cost per unit of output, taking into account the effect on capital, will be reduced.

(iv) The scheme should contain effective controls to ensure that the projected increase in productivity is achieved, and that the payment is made only as productivity increases or as changes in working practice takes place.

(v) The undertaking should be ready to show clear benefits to the consumer through a contribution to stable prices.

(vi) An agreement covering part of an undertaking should bear the cost of consequential increases elsewhere in the same undertaking, if any have to be granted.

(vii) In all cases negotiators should beware of setting extravagant levels of pay which would provoke resentment outside."

These statements make an attempt to distinguish between productivity of labour and other factors, although the question as to how they can be measured is largely left unresolved.[3]

In short, many of the widely publicized discussions of productivity levels have been derived from a basic concern with such larger issues as inflation control, industrial peace and economic growth. As a consequence, it is not surprising that relatively little attention has been given to the seemingly minor issues of how to measure productivity changes, how to determine the means whereby changes have been effected and how to assess their consequences—especially when the answers to such questions have long been assumed to be known. Unfortunately, there is little basis for such blithe assumptions. Moreover, as will be shown, it is precisely because such knowledge has yet to be developed on an authoritative basis that some of our public policies relating to inflation control and to the improvement of industrial performance rest on vulnerable foundations.

The Need for Sounder Productivity Measurement

Our main concern in this study is not with productivity bargaining, but with the problem of measuring the nature and extent of productivity adjustments and their effects. It arose as a result of studies in the analysis of performance within decentralized organizations, where the performance of cost or profit centres needs to be measured in order to facilitate the control and planning of future operations and in order to provide a means of both motivating and judging the performance of the managers concerned. Close analysis of the basic need in such cases emphasizes that the usefulness of any particular measure for a given unit is a function of the specific purpose for which it is constructed, of the nature of the business in which the unit is involved, and the constraints under which the unit exists by virtue of its operation within a decentralized organization rather than independently. Taking the specific evaluative purpose and the specific operational activities into account ensures the *relevance* of the selected measure; regard for the constraints ensures that it will distinguish the variables which are definitely under the *control* of the manager in charge from those subject to decision by others.

As pointed out by Gold [12], widely used concepts of productivity have three serious

---

[3] The contribution of labour to production is not interpreted merely as output per man-hour, but is conditional on the implementation of new or more exacting working practices. There is also an emphasis on price stabilization and the need to consider the interests of the consumer, although again it is not clear how the relationship between price and cost should be handled (see also [15]).

shortcomings:

1. *output per man-hour* does not measure productive efficiency as a whole, or even the productive contributions of labour;
2. increases in output per man-hour may or may not be desirable, and may or may not reduce unit labour costs; and
3. even if increases in output per man-hour are accompanied by only proportionate increases in hourly wage rates, production costs are more likely to increase than to remain unchanged in "capital-dominated" industries, such as the steel industries.

It is therefore clear that an analysis of productivity must be embedded in the cost and profitability structures. The appropriateness of a particular measure reflects the objectives and managerial goals of the unit concerned, which in turn are derived from those of the firm. As is widely recognized, the hierarchy of objectives in the firm produces an organizational structure to pursue them, first by a planning process that specifies an array of activities to be undertaken and allocates resources to them, and secondly by executing the details of the plans. The control function is responsible for monitoring progress, comparing it with targets specified by the plans, taking corrective action when serious discrepancies are revealed and finally undertaking to evaluate the whole planning and execution process when the operations are complete. The purpose of this evaluation is to learn from experience and to show where the process can be improved in future, and an essential part of this learning exercise is to construct a series of measures of performance to guide the analysis, including measures of productivity.

It must therefore be emphasized that guidelines as to *how* to measure productivity may be gained from an analysis of *why* we should wish to measure it. The reasons are fourfold.

(i) *for strategic purposes*, in order to compare the performance of the firm with that of its competitors or related firms, both in terms of aggregate results and in terms of major components of performance;

(ii) *for tactical purposes*, to enable management to control the performance of the firm by identifying the comparative performance of individual sectors of the firm, either by function or by product;

(iii) *for planning purposes*, to compare the relative benefits accruing from the use of different inputs, or varying proportions of the same inputs, currently and over longer periods, as the basis for considering alternative adjustments over future periods; and

(iv) *for other management purposes*, such as collective bargaining with trade unions, assessing the effects of prospective governmental restrictions, etc.

That productivity measures can be used to fulfil so many functions suggests that several types of measures may be appropriate according to the function to be pursued. Thus, when productivity is defined as "a ratio of a measure of output to a measure of some or all of the resources used to produce this output" [7, p. 177], an expansion of such statements is clearly necessary. The phrase "some or all of the resources" introduces an area of confusion into the definition corresponding to the multiplicity of types of inputs. Materials, labour, capital funds, machinery and managerial as well as technical personnel all contribute to the overall output of the firm and hence to changes in input–output relationships. Thus an attempt to measure overall productivity immediately faces the problem of inputs which are heterogeneous and often difficult to measure. In practice, this problem is reflected in the time-consuming efforts which have been devoted to negotiating the division of returns from increases in overall productivity among all of the inputs which have contributed to that increase (or whose non-co-operation could prevent its realization).[4]

The major problems in seeking to apply these seemingly simple elements of productivity analysis centre around:

(a) *measuring output*, especially in the face of changes with time in the design, sizes and types of individual products as well as in the proportions of different product lines;

(b) *measuring inputs*, and accounting for the great multiplicity of types of materials, facilities and equipment usually encountered, as well as the multiplicity of labour and salaried skills to be encompassed—and also in the face of changes in the composition of each of these major input categories over a period of time;

(c) *determining which particular input–output comparisons are most relevant* in evaluating the performance of various operations and units of concern to management; and

(d) *interpreting such findings* with due regard to the need to differentiate between the influence of internally controllable and externally imposed factors.

In view of the importance of these issues, it is not surprising that a considerable body of literature has developed reflecting a variety of approaches to dealing with different parts of this complex domain. A brief review of several of these may help to appreciate the thoughtful and often ingenious efforts which have been devised for overcoming what experience demonstrates are difficulties of quite significant proportions.[5]

Some Alternative Approaches

1. Financial Ratios

One group of contributions reflecting some concern with productivity relationships involves reliance on ratios of financial measures of inputs to financial measures of outputs. Such measures are resorted to as a means of circumventing the problems rooted in the heterogeneity of physical inputs and physical outputs and in the difficulties of assessing the contributions of the different inputs to producing the products in question. By combining the outputs of different products into an aggregate of associated revenues (or profits) and by combining the different inputs into one aggregate of associated outlays or investments, ratios are devised to reflect the financial aspects of productivity relationships.

For example, Risk [23] takes the return on investment as a starting-point and suggests that by dividing assets between departments, the respective ratios of output (at cost) to assets can be used to measure the performance of individual departments or cost centres. Alternatively, return on investment (profit/investment) can be regarded as a function of

---

[4] This has been an especially sore problem in the case of productivity bargains between management and unions. "The judgment must be made on the facts of each case. To lay down a rigid rule of one-third to the worker, one-third to the employer and one-third to the consumer would kill many valuable agreements from the start and permit the exploitation of the consumer in other cases" [19, p. 39].

[5] For a more detailed review see Soesan [28].

operating profitability (profit/revenue) and capital turnover (revenue/investment), and these ratios are further subdivided among component departments.

The practical work of the Centre for Interfirm Comparison in Britain is also based on a pyramid of financial input–financial output ratios as shown in Fig. 1.1: Return on capital, again the key ratio, can be seen to depend on ratios 2 and 3, and these in turn depend on the relationships between sales and profits (and therefore costs, on the left-hand side of the pyramid) and between sales and assets (shown on the right-hand side). The further break-down on the left-hand side represents the proportions of total sales value accounted for by various cost categories. On the right-hand side, the break-down represents the proportions of component categories of assets to the total value of sales. Both sets of ratios can be used, of course, as the basis for setting performance targets and for measuring performance relative to such targets. But the interpretation of such measures of the proportionate composition of costs and of assets as productivity measures obviously reflects a highly specific concern with certain financial aspects of performance, which need not be closely related to the common connotations of the concept of productivity.

2. Productivity Costing Approach

The "productivity costing" approach to measuring productivity emphasizes the contributions to the productivity of a firm of individual products rather than of operating units or functional activities. Thus, the "productivity" of a product is measured by its "efficiency" in making a profit. Bahiri and Martin, the main protagonists of this approach [2, 17, 18], advocate measuring only that work which is truly productive [17], i.e. in relation to the objectives of the organization concerned. The basic assumption is made [18] that an industrial system's operating costs remain essentially stable over the whole normal range of variation of output in the system and that, therefore, once the productive facilities have been identified, productivity can be measured by total earnings of those productive facilities and the rate at which each product generates profit. They construct [2] various productivity indices taking into account all variable expenditure and a minimal overhead apportionment based on optimal facilities usage. The key index is the Product Productivity Index, given by the total earnings of the product over the cost of producing that product. Bahiri and Martin suggest that products can be ranked by means of this index. The break-down of costs used by Bahiri and Martin (see Fig. 1.2) is fundamental to their analysis and determines the structure of their indices. The Product Productivity Index is given by T_d/C_d and a full list of all the productivity indices constructed is given in [2, p. 61]. Tolkowsky [31] notes that productivity costing highlights the costing of manufactured goods, the significance of the degree of utilization of capacity and the impact of idle time on the costs of production.

It is apparent, however, that this approach too reflects a conception less closely associated with the common connotation of "productivity" than with the prevailing business concepts of profit margins by product lines, and of allocations to specified cost categories. As indicated by its designation as "productivity costing", the focus is entirely on costs (and revenue), ignoring underlying physical resource flows and input factor prices.

3. Transfer pricing

Horngren [13] suggests two measures of the productivity of a cost or profit centre: the

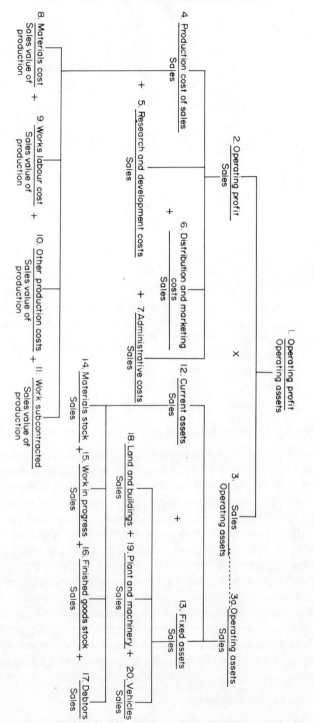

Fig. 1.1. A structure of financial ratios (as advocated by the Centre for Interfirm Comparison [6]).

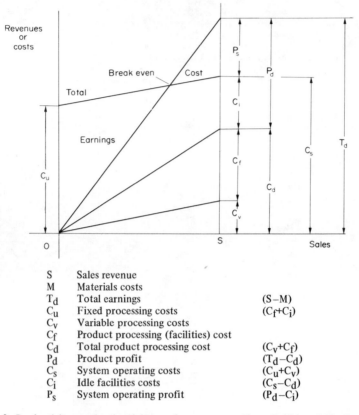

S	Sales revenue	
M	Materials costs	
T_d	Total earnings	$(S-M)$
C_u	Fixed processing costs	(C_f+C_i)
C_v	Variable processing costs	
C_f	Product processing (facilities) cost	
C_d	Total product processing cost	(C_v+C_f)
P_d	Product profit	(T_d-C_d)
C_s	System operating costs	(C_u+C_v)
C_i	Idle facilities costs	(C_s-C_d)
P_s	System operating profit	(P_d-C_i)

Fig. 1.2. Productivity costing breakdown of components (from Bahiri and Martin [2]).

rate of return on investment, and transfer prices. The significance of the rate of return on investment has been discussed above. For tactical or planning purposes, Horngren argues that transfer prices can be used as a measure of "efficiency", if supplying divisions meet all *bona fide* outside price competition and if orders are kept within the company as long as market prices are no less than variable manufacturing costs. This approach is obviously applicable only to firms in which finished products are fairly homogeneous and are transferred from one division to another. Where transfers consist of goods and services produced entirely for internal consumption and not offered for direct sale to the market, transfer prices often lose significance. Even more important for present purposes, transfer prices offer even less direct measures of productivity adjustments than the costs on which they are based (and which have already been reviewed as one of the proposed approaches to productivity measurement). Nor does the requirement of excluding external supplies (unless their prices fall below the internal division's variable manufacturing costs) ensure a much closer relationship between transfer prices and productivity levels, especially in industries with substantial fixed costs and distribution charges.

4. Other empirically oriented approaches

Other approaches to productivity measurement include those of Bowey and Lupton [4], Ball [3], Robertson [24], Amey [1] and Rice [22]. Bowey and Lupton [4] are concerned solely with labour productivity, which they measure by means of seven parameters (e.g. average replacement period for employees) which combine in a set of equations to indicate an optimal pay packet. Ball [3] argues that value added per unit is superior to the rate of return on investment as a measure of the firm's performance because the latter is more responsive to the product price effect of the monopoly position of firms. This opinion is supported by Robertson [24], who cites the case of an engineering firm in which added value is first adjusted to eliminate any changes in selling price, in raw material costs or in cost of outside purchases which have altered since the base period, and then used as a percentage of man-hours for a measure of productivity. Since value added is simply the sum of wages, salaries and gross profits, the ratio of value added to man-hours is none other than the sum of wage (and salary) rate plus the gross profit per man-hour; neither of these tell us very much about productivity. Amey [1] produces similar arguments to those of Ball but suggests unit costs as the best measure. Some links can be seen between his ideas and those of Bahiri and Martin (mentioned earlier). A significant deviation from such approaches is presented in Rice's description of the Ahmedabad Experiment [22], in which productivity is measured by actual output over potential output or by the percentage of output rejected. Here the focus is shifted completely from financial measures (such as profit rates and unit costs) to physical measures, although it is apparent that under-utilization rates may reflect a variety of factors other than what is commonly considered to represent productivity adjustment, especially when attendant cost changes are not accounted for.

Surveys of empirical work in the field of productivity measurements have revealed a number of popular methods for dealing with commonly encountered problems. Easterfield [7] shows, for example, that the problems of multiple inputs have been dealt with largely by reducing them to a common measure (imputed man-hours, costs, imputed capital value) or by constructing a production function relating the various inputs.

Other interesting efforts include the use by the British Ship Research Association of. a measure of output more elaborate than merely the weight of the ships, to allow for the varying work content per ton of steel of different types of ships. They, therefore, determine the standard work content and corresponding man-hours of a basic notional ship to be used as a yardstick. The factors of other ships are then related to that of the notional ship. The actual gross steel weight of the ship multiplied by its comparison factor then gives the "equivalent gross steel weight" which, when divided into total steelwork man-hours, gives a steelwork productivity index. These indexes have been used for comparative purposes at shipyards throughout the country [5].

Some interesting work has also been done in the shipbuilding industry in Japan. A major argument produced in favour of modernizing the industry by fabricating larger component units before assembly is an estimated reduction in man-hours at the shipyard of over 80 per cent [30, p. 59]. The increase in labour productivity has been estimated for each job at each stage of manufacture. More detailed work has also been done on the quality as well as the productivity of the welding process in shipbuilding [29]. This work is certainly useful in the context of the shipbuilding industry, but has its limitations when attempts are made to apply it in other industries.

Nevertheless, it is interesting, given an ever-increasing public awareness of the subject of productivity, how few attempts have been made to measure it in practice. Even a study of the reports of the National Board for Prices and Incomes (in Britain), whose prime concern was to ensure that increases in pay were matched by increases in productivity, revealed only isolated attempts to actually measure the latter. The Board appears to have adopted a fairly simple-minded approach to the problem of productivity measurement, when it tackled it at all, being satisfied with such measures as average output per operative hour, without further definition, in industries as diverse as engineering and icecream manufactufe [20, 21].

Since its foundation in 1959, the Centre of Interfirm Comparisons in Britain has prepared or conducted comparisons of productivity and profitability in some sixty industries, ranging from heavy engineering to stockbrokers, from biscuit manufacture to cotton spinning. The comparison is based on the pyramid of management ratios shown in Fig. 1.1 in addition to data on production, research and development, capital investment, marketing, warehousing and distribution, administration and financial structure.

Relevant work by the British Trades Union Congress and the Engineering Employers' Federation has naturally concentrated on labour productivity, particularly since the initiation of productivity bargaining with the Fawley Agreement in 1960. However, in all cases the amount of work done in this field is disappointing, perhaps because of the very nature of productivity bargaining. Since these normally cover a specific innovation or change, the only calculations necessary relate to the cost savings to be expected as a result of that change rather than to the levels of productivity before and after the change takes place.

5. Other general approaches

Farrell [9] has attempted to measure the "technical efficiency" of a productive unit through the concept of an "efficient production function". Suppose a production system produces a single output from two inputs; the locus of all points of the most efficient way of producing a given output from combinations of the two inputs is called the "efficient production function" and is shown as line EBE' in Fig. 1.3. All points on this curve are said to be equally efficient, while point A is said to be less efficient, since it requires more inputs than, say, point B for the production of the same output. The ratio OB/OA may then be regarded as a quantitative measure of the efficiency of a system operating at point A. This method can easily be extended to a multi-input–single-output case, or to that involving single-input–multi-output.

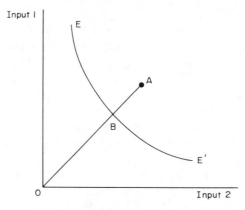

Fig. 1.3. Farrell's technical efficiency of two-input/single-output firms [9].

Farrell's method suffers from two main shortcomings. First, it is not extendable in its simple form to the multi-input–multi-output case, which–after all–is the most commonly found in industry. Secondly, there are serious theoretical and practical difficulties in constructing the "efficient production function", except in very simple or trivial cases. Even when there are no ambiguities in the definition and measurement of inputs and outputs, a sufficiently large number of points describing individual operating systems needs to be assembled before a lower bounding envelope (which is then interpreted as the "most efficient") can be drawn. Indeed, an empirical investigation of eleven 2-input, single-output plants did not produce very promising results [25].

A variety of efforts have also been made to use operational research techniques in approaching productivity analysis. In general, mathematical programming can be employed to find the critical limiting factors in any given productive process. This modelling technique is generally concerned with the optimization of a single objective function, which either reflects a single objective specified by management or a weighted sum of several objectives. The method can be adapted for use in a "satisficing" mode with the view of achieving minimum levels of pre-specified performance measures which are considered to be "good enough" [8]. Whichever approach is adopted, an analysis of the goals involved clearly implies knowledge and use of productivity ratios or costing techniques and can in turn be used to guide management in its control of the critical variables in the production process.

A variant to the single objective function approach in mathematical programming is the goal programming formulation proposed by Ijiri [14]. He starts with a set of desirable goals or targets associated with defined measures of performance, some financial, others physical, and proceeds to measure the extent to which these targets are "missed": "underages" in the case of short falls and "overages" when the targets are exceeded. He then constructs an objective function of weighted overages and underages, so that when the function is minimized, a solution is obtained as close as possible to the given set of goals.

A major merit of this goal-programming approach is that it highlights the critical constraining variables in the system and thereby directs the attention of the manager to the area of greatest concern. The disadvantage of the method lies in the fact that the goals (be they expressed in terms of outputs, inputs, use of plant, or financial ratios) are essentially arbitrary and reflect a desire to relate to some past performance criteria or to heed certain constraints imposed on the system. The problem of comparing the performance of two units remains unresolved, unless specific performance measures are defined, including a ranking or weighting procedure to reduce all such measures to a single denominator. Goal programming may, therefore, be regarded as a useful planning tool, but it is not very amenable to measuring productivity.

Conclusions

In short, a review of published studies of productivity adjustments reveals widespread differences concerning the nature of productivity gains, the effective means of measuring them and the evaluation of their effects. The most pervasive concept of productivity associates it closely with the technological concept of efficiency as revealed by changes in the level of output derived from a given volume of inputs. Setting aside these essentially physical-input–physical-output relationships, others have emphasized that with respect to economic activities, changes in physical *efficiency* must be appraised in terms of resulting adjustments in the *economy* of the process, as reflected in measures such as unit costs. Still others stress that changes in *profitability* are the over-riding criteria in evaluations of adjustments in performance.

It is obvious, of course, that such diverse conceptions tend to produce disparate findings. But it is also clear that each is relevant and, indeed, significant. Accordingly, one is led to recognize the need for a multi-dimensional analytical framework to encompass variations in a multi-dimensional process. And inasmuch as all measurements depend on the purposes to be fulfilled, progress in productivity measurement also requires clarification of the objectives guiding such efforts, as well as recognition that different purposes are likely to require comparably differentiated measures.

Accordingly, Chapter 2 will suggest concepts, an analytical framework and an array of measures oriented to specified purposes; this analysis has been applied to increasingly complex and more highly aggregated industrial operations as a test of its usefulness for practical managerial planning and for evaluation of performance, and several illustrative case studies are described in Chapters 4-6.

References

1. Amey, L. R. (1964) The allocation and utilization of resources. *Operational Research Quarterly*, vol. 15, no. 2, pp. 87-100.
2. Bahiri, S. and Martin, H. W. (1970) Productivity costing and management. *Management International Review*, vol. 10, no. 1, pp. 55-77.
3. Ball, R. J. (1968) The use of value added in measuring managerial efficiency. *Business Ratios*, Summer vol., pp. 3-9.
4. Bowey, A. M. and Lupton, T. (1970) Productivity drift and the structure of the pay packet. *Journal of Management Studies*, vol. 7, no. 2, pp. 156-71 and no. 3, pp. 310-34.
5. British Ship Research Association (1963) Productivity index for steelwork. *Technical Memorandum* 169.
6. Centre for Interfirm Comparison (1968) Published accounts: your yardsticks of performance?
7. Easterfield, T. E. (1959) *Productivity Measurement in Great Britain*. Department of Scientific and Industrial Research, U.K.
8. Eilon, S. (1972) Goals and constraints in decision making. *Operational Research Quarterly*, vol. 23, no. 1, pp. 3-15.
9. Farrell, M. J. (1957) The measurement of productive efficiency. *Journal of the Royal Statistical Society*, Series A, vol. 120, part III, pp. 253-90.
10. Flanders, A. (1964) *The Fawley Productivity Agreement*. Faber, London.
11. Furst, G., Raabe, K. H. and Sperling, H. (1962) Output per person employed in the major sectors of the German economy. *Productivity Measurement Review*, OECD.
12. Gold, B. (1974) Productivity analyses, some new analytical and empirical perspectives. *Business Economics*, vol. 9, no. 3, pp. 64-65.
13. Horngren, C. T. (1965) *Accounting for Management Control: an Introduction*. Prentice-Hall, Englewood Cliffs, NJ.
14. Ijiri, Y. (1965) *Management Goals and Accounting for Control*. North-Holland, Amsterdam.
15. Kaplan, A. D. H., Dirlam, J. B. and Lanzillotti, R. F. (1958) *Pricing in Big Business*. The Brookings Institution, Washington, D.C.
16. *London Gazette* (26 August 1966) Notice on productivity agreements with references to the Prices and Incomes Act, 1966.
17. Martin, H. W. (1959) Towards a common measure of productivity. *Productivity Measurement Review*, OEEC, vol. 19, November, pp. 5-30.
18. Martin, H. W. (1964) Productivity costing and control. *Productivity Measurement Review*, OECD, vol. 37, May, pp. 12-76.
19. National Board for Prices and Incomes (1967) *Productivity Agreements*, Cmnd 3311. HMSO, London.

20. National Board for Prices and Incomes (1968) *Pay and Conditions of Service of Engineering Workers*, Cmnd 3495. HMSO, London.
21. National Board for Prices and Incomes (1970) *Costs, Prices and Profitability in the Ice-cream Manufacturing Industry*, Cmnd 4548, HMSO, London.
22. Rice, A. K. (1970) *Productivity and Social Organisation.* Tavistock, London.
23. Risk, J. M. S. (1965) Productivity yardsticks. *Management Accounting* U.K., vol. 43, no. 11, pp. 381-91.
24. Robertson, E. J. (1968) Productivity bargaining and the engineering industry. Federation Research Paper 1, Engineering Employers' Federation, U.K.
25. Sahgal, B. (1972) Measures of productivity and efficiency—an empirical study. M.Sc. report, Imperial College, London.
26. Smith, E. O. (1971) *Productivity Bargaining, a Case Study in the Steel Industry.* Pan Books, London.
27. Smith, I. G. (1973) *The Measurement of Productivity.* Gower Press, London.
28. Soesan, J. (1975) *Productivity Measurement.* Ph.D. thesis, to be submitted to the University of London.
29. Terai, K. (1970) *Present Status of Welding in Shipbuilding.* Kawasaki Heavy Industries Ltd., Kobe, Japan.
30. Terai, K. and Kurioka, T. (1969) *Future Shipbuilding Methods.* Kawasaki Heavy Industries Ltd., Kobe, Japan.
31. Tolkowsky, D. (1964) Productivity costing: a comment on its practical applications. *Productivity Measurement Review*, OECD, vol. 37, pp. 9-12.

CHAPTER 2

A Framework for Productivity Analysis

BELA GOLD

1. Objectives

As has already been mentioned, changes in productivity levels are increasingly recognized as a major influence on a wide range of managerial problems, including wage levels, cost-price relationships, capital investment requirements, labour utilization and even competitive standing. The very importance of these problems, however, emphasizes the seriousness of continued widespread misunderstanding of the nature and effects of productivity adjustments.

Among the most widely prevailing elements of the mythology relating to productivity, the following four may be most important:

1. that productivity measures reflect changes in the "efficiency" of production;
2. that changes in productivity are reasonably well measured by output per man-hour;
3. that increases in output per man-hour are invariably desirable because they yield decreases in unit costs; and
4. that increases in output per man-hour warrant parallel increases in wages per man-hour.

And yet, not one of these contentions can be sustained either on theoretical or on empirical grounds, as will be shown. In order to help redirect the analysis of productivity adjustments, it is necessary:

1. to clarify the *nature* of productivity adjustments;
2. to develop more effective *measures* of changes in productivity;
3. to explore the *sources* of significant changes in productivity;
4. to trace the successive linkages whereby productivity adjustments *affect* costs, prices and profitability; and
5. to *integrate* all of the foregoing *into a managerial control system* designed to enable management:
    (a) to appraise alternative means of changing productivity;
    (b) to appraise managerial alternatives in the application of such innovations; and
    (c) to determine the effects of past as well as of prospective innovations.

It is also necessary to recognize at the outset that productivity adjustments can only be appraised within some specified framework which encompasses all input-output flows of the system and which also specifies the criteria in terms of which alternatives are considered and performance evaluated. Although the primary focus of this study will be

16

on productivity analysis within the firm as viewed by management, it is apparent that such analyses may also be needed from other points of view and at other levels of aggregation.

2. Nature of Productivity Adjustments

Many of the limitations of productivity analysis are traceable to the effects of its early development in agricultural and simple manufacturing processes. The shifting of such efforts from relatively primitive production operations to highly complex activity systems, and from the context of engineering measurements of physical relationships to that of managerial appraisals of economic relationships, requires far-reaching readjustments in purposes, concepts and methods which have often been overlooked [8].

It is a striking anomaly that acceptance of productivity as an important measure of economic performance has grown simultaneously with the declining relevance of its common meanings to modern economic processes. One of these meanings derives from the agricultural concept of relative fertility and reflects differences in the output potentials of equal-sized plots of land (actual yields being expected to fluctuate in all plots with weather changes). Because such differences are attributed to the unequal natural endowments of the plots, this particular input is regarded as the active or creative agent in determining output differentials, while other inputs are viewed as essentially passive. The other common meaning of productivity derives from the engineering concept of efficiency and reflects the relationship between the actual and the potential output for any process, as may be illustrated by the percentage of the energy potential of fuels actually converted into brake horsepower or other forms of energy output by an engine.

Differences between the "input creativity" and the "conversion efficiency" concepts of productivity are important enough to warrant reviewing them in some detail. Specifically, the conversion concept shifts the focus of analysis from disparities in performance potentials among different systems to changes in the proportion of each system's potentials actually utilized; it shifts the scope of measurement from comparing total output with one input to comparing it with total input; and it shifts the basis for explaining productivity changes from the creativity of active inputs (for these would alter the system's potentials) to the effectiveness of the conversion process, which embodies engineering (and perhaps managerial) contributions to system performance. Incidentally, the latter also illustrates attendant differences in interpretive viewpoints between farm owners and process engineers concerning what is important and, therefore, to be measured. Another important difference is that the input creativity approach emphasizes the non-comparability of inputs and outputs, whereas the conversion efficiency approach stresses the reduction of both to common terms (e.g. British thermal unit equivalents) —thus limiting fertility comparisons to systems with similar inputs and similar outputs, whereas relative efficiency levels may be compared among quite dissimilar mass and energy conversion systems (e.g. thermal, mechanical and electrical).

Despite such sharp distinctions, prevailing concepts of the nature of productivity adjustments reflect a strange mixture of both approaches, thus sharing the limitations of each and highlighting the conflicts between them. This has come about partly because the development of economic activity systems has endowed most of them with characteristics associated with both these primitive concepts, and partly because differences among

17

interest groups have encouraged comparably polarized approaches.

Each of these concepts of productivity adjustments is weakened by its myopic concentration on one component of a complex of relationships. By attributing increases in total output per unit of a given input to improvements in the qualitative contributions of that factor, the input creativity concept implies that there have been no changes in: (a) the nature and composition of output; (b) the volume, quality and utilization of each of the other inputs; and (c) the nature of production processes. By attributing input–output adjustments solely to processing innovations which reduce the wastage of inputs, or increase the effectiveness with which processes harness the potential contributions of inputs, the conversion efficiency concept likewise implies no attendant changes in other conditions. Moreover, the general conclusion in each case that increases in output–input ratios are economically beneficial rests on the further assumption that factor and product prices are unchanged. In each case, therefore, the interpretation may be valid only when all of these implied conditions are satisfied.

Reasonable approximations to such restrictive conditions do, of course, occur. The former may be illustrated by increases in butter output due to the use of richer milk, and the latter by increases in heat produced from unchanged inputs through improved combustion conditions in the same furnace. But such cases tend to be increasingly uncommon because modern economic systems tend to generate unceasing pressures for improvements both through changing products, processes and inputs and through improving their adjustments to one another. Indeed, the original fertility concept has become inadequate even in respect to agriculture in view of the responsiveness of yields to improved seeds, more fertilizer, farm machinery and pesticides. And the original conversion efficiency concept has become inadequate even in respect to most processing innovations because of their tendency to alter the quality and relative quantities of various inputs and, often, of outputs as well.

The widespread confusion resulting from the application of such primitive concepts to modern industry may be illustrated at three levels. At the level of basic concepts, one may note that productivity adjustments are usually measured by comparing total output with one input, as in the input creativity approach; but results are interpreted as indicating changes in the efficiency of the process—although output per man-hour, for example, cannot measure variations in the productive efficiency of most industrial operations, nor in the efficiency of labour efforts alone, nor even in the sheer magnitude of labour's contributions to output (which would be more closely akin to the input creativity concept). At the level of interpreting findings, each input group's view of itself as the sole source of creative gains in productivity, despite the active involvement of other inputs in modern production adjustments, often leads to simultaneous claims by several groups for credit in accounting for observed gains in output–input ratios (and to unembarrassed reversals of the same arguments in blaming unfavourable adjustments on other factors). And at the level of appraisal, the general, but unwarranted, assumption that all improvements in input–output ratios are necessarily beneficial may be traced back to these primitive conceptions that such gains can only be due to the enhanced creativity of inputs, to reduced wastage of inputs, or to process improvements which more fully harness the productive potentials of inputs.

To analyse the complex domain of input–output relationships in modern industry, however, it is necessary to broaden the concept of the nature of productivity adjustments to include the effects of changes: in the quality and degree of utilization of any or all inputs, as well as in the quantitative proportions of various inputs; and in the qualitative characteristics of each product as well as in the quantitative proportions of different products. As a result, three new problems of measurement must be dealt with: how to combine different product (or input) flows into meaningful aggregates; how to deal with qualitative changes in particular inputs or outputs through time; and how to keep input and output measurements independent of one another.

3. Requirements of Productivity Analysis

The absence of a unitary concept of efficiency which is widely applicable means that productivity studies in modern economies cannot undertake to measure the efficiency of a given activity system. Instead, such studies must be designed to appraise the effects of changes in various input-output relationships on specified performance objectives of the system, thus shifting from a descriptive to an analytical viewpoint. Inasmuch as different activity systems are likely to have different objectives, and each system is likely to have a variety of performance criteria—as will be discussed in greater detail later—it follows that each system may be characterized by an array of productivity relationships at any given time and also that identical measurements may have widely disparate meanings in different systems. This does not mean that there is anything especially subtle about the process of productivity measurement [19], but only that the variety of relationships is so great that making effective choices requires defining the particular activity sectors to be probed and the criteria to be applied.

It also follows that merely juxtaposing the comparative magnitudes of specified inputs and outputs reveals nothing more than the level of, or changes in, the given ratio. To evaluate such quantitative findings, the variables should be derived from an analytical framework which encompasses all of the inputs and outputs of the system and provides a theory of how it functions.[1] Such a framework permits working backward from specified performance objectives to determine which variables should be studied, how they should be related to one another, and what measurements should be used for each in order to make most effective use of resulting findings. Accordingly, productivity measurements cannot provide the basis for a theory of the determinants of effectiveness in marketing, education [3, pp. 19-28], or research [16]; on the contrary, such theories are pre-requisites for determining the elements and structure of input-output measurements which are meaningful for evaluating the performance of these systems. In general, then, the less rigorous and detailed the analytical framework used, the less significant may be the measures contrived and the more vulnerable the interpretations attempted, as has been amply illustrated by indiscriminate reliance on output per man-hour measures over a wide range of economic activities.

The significance of given input-output ratios depends not only on the analytical relevance of the categories used, but on five additional requirements whose intuitive recognition in simple production systems has often been overlooked in other applications. Two of these concern the qualitative stability of each input and output category through time and the susceptibility to measurement of those attributes which bear directly on the

[1] A widely accepted contrasting view is expressed by Solow [18]: "The economist really need not know at all what it feels like to be inside a steel plant ... he quantifies technological change by making measurements of output per man-hour, or output per unit of this or input per unit of that."

evaluative criteria being employed. The former emphasizes that changes in the inputs or outputs may confuse interpretation of observed adjustments in quantitative input–output relationships, as may be illustrated by changes in the productivity of smelters traceable to variations in the metal content of ores. And the second warns of the dangers of quantifying peripheral rather than core aspects of input and output flows, as may be illustrated by the common use of tonnage shipped to measure the output of steel mills, although most production efforts beyond the furnaces seek to increase the value of products by changing the shape, and incidentally reducing the weight, of the steel being processed.

The three remaining requirements are that the numerator and denominator of productivity ratios should relate to congruent sectors of activity; that they should relate to properly linked time periods; and that the contribution of the input must be absorbed into, and affect, the output. In emphasizing that the inputs and outputs being compared must relate to the same department, plant, firm or industry, the first requirement merely seeks to prevent such errors as comparing all of the inputs of a plant with only part of its output (e.g. relating total man-hours in an integrated steel mill to the ingot tonnage output of the furnaces). The second counsels against using input and output data for the same period unless all of the input is absorbed into the output within that period. Thus, in an operation involving a 6-month production cycle, it may be more meaningful to compare output levels with the material consumption levels of 6 months earlier than with their current levels. The direct implication of the third requirement is that outputs should be compared with input measurements covering all of the factors which can be substituted for one another. To illustrate: it would be easy to misinterpret changes in the ratio of pig-iron input to open-hearth steel output if no account were taken of corresponding changes in the scrap-steel inputs which may be used in place of pig iron.

Finally, the uses to be made of productivity findings may generate additional requirements bearing on the design of effective measures. For example, efforts to determine the economic significance of changes in physical input–output relationships, or the physical bases for changes in economic relationships, may require a superstructure of additional measures, as will be shown later. And if appraisal efforts are also to be directed towards the managerial objectives of improvement and control, productivity measures might be redesigned so as to maximize the separation of components which are responsive to managerial guidance from those which are not.

4. Productivity Analysis and Managerial Performance Criteria

But no firm is dominated by the objective of maximizing physical output relative to physical inputs. Hence, if one is to understand productivity adjustments in actual industrial operations, it is necessary to develop a framework which reflects the hierarchy of pressures which shapes managerial decision-making and performance evaluation [7;9, chaps. 2 and 8].

Efforts to dig beneath the final measure of business performance represented by the rate of profit on investment have long been dominated by various sets of financial ratios. Relationships among items in the income statement and balance-sheet seem to have been developed into tools for appraising the soundness of the underlying structure by prospective lenders and investors. The influence of these viewpoints on capital markets and on

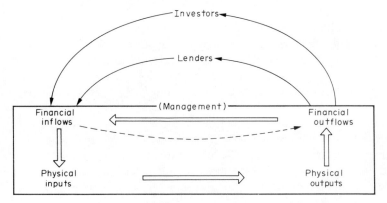

Fig. 2.1. Physical and financial resource flows within the firm.

corporate financial officers has ensured continued reliance on such diagnostic tools and even their further elaboration. Like other special purpose tools, however, their usefulness drops off rapidly when forced into alien tasks. And the responsibilities of operating management are sufficiently different from those of lenders and investors to require a comparably differentiated structure of evaluative criteria.

Figure 2.1 helps to clarify some of these differences. It shows business activity as a four-stage process consisting of inflows of financial resources from investors and lenders, the conversion of these into physical inputs, the transformation of such inputs into physical outputs, and the conversion of physical goods and services through sales into financial outflows, which are allocated to lenders and investors, and fed back into the business. Investors and lenders virtually monopolize the upper, or financial, level of these flows–substituting for the actual conversions into physical resources and eventually back into financial flows (see broken line).

The financial ratios favoured by suppliers of funds depend, of course, on the nature of their involvements. Short-term lenders are understandably preoccupied with the security of their commitments as reflected by such ratios as current assets to current liabilities, inventories to sales and net working capital to sales. Long-term lenders are similarly concerned with the security of their resources, as reflected by such ratios as sales to fixed investment and long-term debt to net worth. Similarly, investors concentrate on the relationships between financial inflows and outflows which affect their prospective shares, as measured by such ratios as profit to total investment and to equity investment. But all of these interests are encompassed by the financial level of flows and, therefore, financial evaluations dominate the annual reports of corporate performance from which these ratios are determined.

And in order to help identify the sources of observed adjustments in the results reported in financial statements, many top managements use variants of the common ratios reflecting differences in the subdivision of total costs and of total investment [12, 13, 20]. For example, DuPont emphasizes Profit/Sales, Sales/Total Investment, and Profit/ Total Investment as well as the composition of cost of sales, of working capital and of total investment [15]. Monsanto concentrates on Profit/Investment, Net Income/ Investment, Sales/Property and the ratios of selling expense, operating expense and cost of goods sold to sales [4]. Armstrong Cork and West Virginia Pulp and Paper have used

21

essentially similar patterns [1].

Although committed to certain of the same objectives as investors, operating management's primary responsibilities centre around the adjustment of the level and composition of the physical inputs and outputs through which financial inflows are converted into larger financial returns. Thus, as indicated in Fig. 2.1, management requires criteria of performance relating financial outlays to physical input quantities, physical output quantities to physical input quantities, and the financial value of outputs to their physical volume. Such measures parallel the sequential processes starting with the conversion of investment funds into physical input flows through the price and quantity commitments of procurement and hiring staff in material, capital goods and labour markets. These are transformed into a flow of products through production and assembly operations. And such physical output is converted into a revenue flow through sales efforts leading to price and quantity commitments in product markets.

In addition, management needs sufficient elaboration of this network at various levels of activity to differentiate between short-term and longer-term determinants of aggregate performance, and between internally controlled and externally imposed adjustments. Finally, management requires the extension of such an integrated structure of performance criteria to progressively lower levels of organizational activity.

The resulting framework would help to trace changes in aggregate levels of performance back through intervening linkages to the initiating units. It would guide efforts to explore the likely ramifications of prospective changes in specified operations. Moreover, it would assist planning by specifying the magnitudes of component adjustments necessary to achieve proposed aggregate advances, and by highlighting the interactions likely to be triggered by prospective innovations.

In accordance with common practice, the present analysis will begin with the assumption that management's primary measure of aggregate performance is the rate of profit on investment. This assumption is wholly incorrect, of course, if it is emphasized to the exclusion of all other objectives [5, chaps. 4 and 7, pp. 272-88]. The areas of decision-making which affect this objective may be identified by proceeding through the five simple stages of analysis reviewed below. The ratio of profit (before tax) to total investment may be regarded as determined by the ratio of profit to physical output and by the ratio of output to total investment:

$$\frac{\text{Profit}}{\text{Total Investment}} \equiv \frac{\text{Profit}}{\text{Output}} \times \frac{\text{Output}}{\text{Total Investment}} \qquad (2.1)$$

But profit per unit of output is determined by the difference between the average gross receipts per unit of output (i.e. average realised price) and average total costs per unit of output:

$$\frac{\text{Profit}}{\text{Output}} \equiv \underset{\text{(average price)}}{\frac{\text{Value of Products}}{\text{Output}}} - \underset{\text{(average unit cost)}}{\frac{\text{Total Costs}}{\text{Output}}} \qquad (2.2)$$

In seeking the determinants of changes in the ratio of output to total investment (the final ratio in (2.1)), one may follow the process whereby the latter is linked to the former. Specifically, part of total investment is allocated to facilities and equipment which determine productive capacity and it is the latter which determines output potentials. Hence, changes in the ratio of output to total investment may be regarded as determined by the ratios of output to productive capacity, of productive capacity to fixed investment, and of fixed investment to total investment:

$$\frac{\text{Output}}{\text{Total Investment}} \equiv \underbrace{\frac{\text{Output}}{\text{Capacity}}}_{\substack{\text{(utilization} \\ \text{rate)}}} \times \underbrace{\frac{\text{Capacity}}{\text{Fixed Investment}}}_{\substack{\text{(productivity of} \\ \text{fixed investment)}}} \times \underbrace{\frac{\text{Fixed Investment}}{\text{Total Investment}}}_{\substack{\text{(internal allocation} \\ \text{of capital)}}} \quad (2.3)$$

Thus, changes in the ratio of profit to total investment may be attributed to five areas of performance: product prices (Total Product Value/Output); unit costs (Total Costs/Output); utilization of facilities (Output/Capacity); productivity of facilities and equipment (Capacity/Fixed Investment); and the allocation of investment resources between capital goods and working capital (Fixed Investment/Total Investment):

$$\frac{\text{Profit}}{\text{Total Investment}} \equiv \left(\frac{\text{Product Value}}{\text{Output}} - \frac{\text{Total Costs}}{\text{Output}} \right) \times$$

$$\times \frac{\text{Output}}{\text{Capacity}} \times \frac{\text{Capacity}}{\text{Fixed Investment}} \times \frac{\text{Fixed Investment}}{\text{Total Investment}} \quad (2.4)$$

Moreover, a shift in focus to the ratio of profit to equity investment would add a sixth area of decision making concerned with the structure of financing:

$$\frac{\text{Profit}}{\text{Equity Investment}} = \frac{\text{Profit}}{\text{Total Investment}} \div \frac{\text{Equity Investment}}{\text{Total Investment}} \quad (2.5)$$

Useful bases for the planning and evaluation efforts of top management seem to be provided by these six managerial control ratios, for they represent a blend of physical and financial aspects of resource flows, of short- and long-term perspectives, and of the stock and flow components of the system. Specifically, since capacity, fixed and total investment tend to change very much more slowly than sales (or value of product), costs and output, the first three ratios in (2.4) would tend to determine short-term changes in Profit/Total Investment. Long-term changes in the latter would be traceable, in turn, not only to the remaining two control ratios, but also to persistent trends in the first three. Both the physical and financial aspects of stock and flows are accordingly encompassed. The differences between these managerial control ratios and commonly used financial analysis ratios are shown in Fig. 2.2 [9, pp. 25-27, 161-5].

Application of this network of managerial control ratios to the performance records of particular firms or plants can reveal which of the strategic areas of decision-making contributed most or least to observed adjustments in the rate of profits on investment.[2]

[2] For illustrative empirical findings see [9, pp. 172-3].

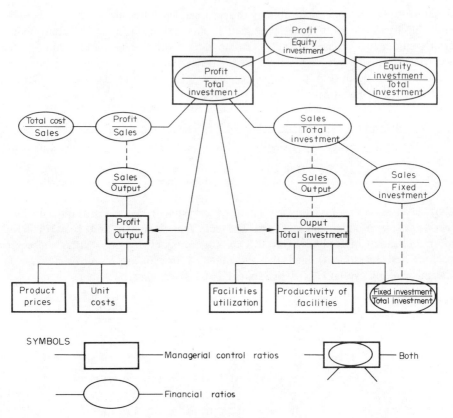

Fig. 2.2. Comparison of managerial control and financial ratios.

Moreover, if the analysis is applied to records covering a long period, the findings may be expected to reveal any persistent trends in the sources of upward and downward pressures on the rate of returns, and also to spotlight the sectors most likely to shift between exercising favourable and unfavourable effects.

This analytical framework may also be used in forward planning to help analyse either the probable effects of expected changes on the rate of return or the alternative combinations of adjustments needed to achieve specified profits (see Chapter 8). Accordingly, in analysing productivity adjustment alternatives and effects, it must always be borne in mind that:

1. top management seeks not to maximize performance within each subsector of operations, but rather to effect the best combination of such component performances—those which most effectively reinforce one another in promoting the objectives of the firm;

2. hence, management must consider alternative patterns of price, output, investment and productivity adjustments instead of concentrating on productivity improvement efforts alone; and

3. actual or prospective adjustments in physical input–physical output relationships must, therefore, be appraised within such a larger analytical framework to yield evaluations relevant to managerial decision-making.

24

5. Characteristics of Productivity Networks

Even casual examination of modern industries demonstrates that output per man-hour measures neither the efficiency of production operations as a whole nor the efficiency of labour's own efforts. Production usually involves integrating the contributions of many kinds of materials and purchased supplies, a variety of labour skills, numerous types of capital facilities and equipment and a wide array of technical and managerial efforts in order to fabricate a range of products. Appraisals of the efficiency of this entire complex of activities must obviously encompass all of the inputs and outputs. But output per man-hour ignores all inputs but one, thereby encouraging gross errors both in evaluating the effects of changes in this measure and in using it to appraise the desirability of prospective innovations.

In order to meet the requirements of practical decision-making by management, productivity analysis must be transformed so as to cover:

(a) changes in the level of each category of input requirements per unit of output, including materials, facilities investment and salaried personnel as well as direct labour;

(b) changes in the proportions in which inputs are combined, both in order to take account of substitutions (e.g. buying more highly fabricated components instead of making them, or replacing labour with machinery) and also in order to differentiate between changes in the productivity of major as over against minor inputs;

(c) differences between the productivity of inputs when they are fully utilized and when their contributions are reduced by idleness; and

(d) variations in all components of this "network of productivity relationships" as viewed simultaneously by managers capable of adjusting relationships among them in the interests of improving aggregate performance relative to specified criteria.

One means of meeting these needs is offered by the following model covering direct inputs (Fig. 2.3). It identifies six components of the network of productivity relationships. Three cover the input requirements per unit of output not only for labour, but also for materials and for fixed capital. In the case of the latter, net fixed investment is compared with productive capacity rather than with output in order to differentiate between what the capital goods can produce and the extent to which they are under-utilized because of market factors [6, pp. 64-6]. The remaining three links cover the proportions in which

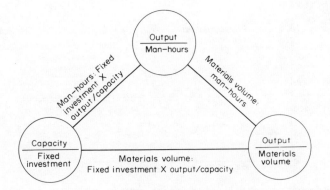

Fig. 2.3. The network of productivity relationships among direct input factors [9].

25

these are combined, e.g. the extent to which more highly processed materials or additional facilities may be substituted for labour. Because of the possibility noted above that capital facilities may be under-utilized, these factor proportions relate labour and materials inputs to "actively utilized" net fixed investment [6, p. 174].

By presenting productivity relationships as a network of interactions, this approach emphasizes that a change in any component, such as output per man-hour, may be merely the *passive* resultant of changes initiated elsewhere in the network, because all components must be brought back into balance. For example, the partial displacement of labour by additional machines would represent an initiating impact on the ratio of man-hours to actively utilized facilities and would lead to increased output per man-hour, even if the remaining labour continued to work at unchanged tasks and at an unchanged pace. But the adjustment process would not yet be complete. The increase in output per man-hour would require either a reduction in man-hours, if output remained at the earlier level, or an increase in materials inputs to permit the maintenance of total man-hours by increasing output in proportion to the gain in output per man-hour. In either case, the ratio of man-hours to materials inputs would decline—thus completing the adjustment cycle on the assumption that the originating replacement of labour by additional machines involved no change in materials requirements per unit of output or in the ratio of capacity to fixed investment [11, p. 65].

Of course, output per man-hour may rise for a variety of reasons other than increased effort by direct labour. Among these may be mentioned the *reduction of labour's contributions* through: the purchase of more highly fabricated components; the replacement of manual tasks by machinery; and the shifting of product-mix in favour of those requiring less manpower. Still another set of innovations might *increase output without expanding labour's contributions* through expanding the output of given machinery or facilities without changing the numbers tending it—either by utilizing machine capacity more fully, or by increasing its capacity through technical innovations.

Such changes in the "apparent productivity" of direct inputs and in their proportions may be illustrated by the U.S. Basic Iron and Steel Industry during 1904-69 (Fig. 2.4). Because this is a "capital-dominated" industry, with labour's role largely restricted to

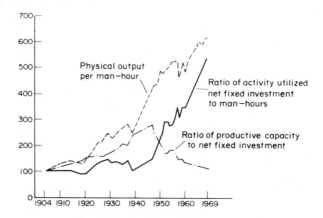

Fig. 2.4. Physical output per man-hour, productive capacity relative to net fixed investment and actively utilized net fixed investment relative to man-hours for U.S. basic steel industry 1904-69, 1904=100.

26

tending equipment in accordance with technically determined procedures, changes in output per man-hour are compared with the productive capacity per dollar of net fixed investment provided by capital facilities and with the ratio of man-hours to the actively utilized portion of the facilities embodying the net fixed investment. Figure 2.4 shows four sub-periods with markedly different relationships: two in which the increase in output per man-hour was associated primarily with increases in the ratio of utilized net investment to man-hours (1921-9 and 1947-69); and two in which the increase in output per man-hour was associated primarily with the ratio of capacity to net fixed investment. This leaves no period in which the primary contribution to rising output per man-hour seemed attributable to intensified labour efforts (Table 2.1).[3]

Table 2.1

	Output Man-hours (%)	Capacity Net fixed investment (%)	Utilized net fixed investment Man-hours (%)
1904-21	+46	+57	− 8
1921-29	+69	+ 7	+60
1929-47	+73	+70	+ 2
1947-69	+45	−60	+265

In short, in using this model of the network of productivity relationships it is necessary to identify the source of the innovational impact instead of assuming that it was engendered within any component registering a change. It is also necessary to trace the effects of an initiating impact in any component through the adaptive adjustments necessitated in the other components of the integrated process, subject both to market constraints and to the technological constraints depending on whether the production activities involved are "labour-dominated", "capital-dominated" or "materials-dominated", as will be discussed later.

6. "Productivity Networks", "Cost Structure" and "Managerial Control Ratios"

Whatever may be the technological desiderata of engineers, however, the appraisal of innovations from the economic point of view—which is critical for managerial purposes—cannot be restricted to predominantly physical input–output relationships. Specifically, management cannot evaluate the net benefits of a past innovation solely on the basis of data specifying resulting adjustments in each of the six components of the network of productivity relationships. Nor can management choose between alternative innovations on the basis solely of estimated effects on each of these six components. Estimates of such relationships are critical elements in appraising their economic implications, but the analysis must be extended to include the latter if it is to serve as a sound basis for

[3] Incidentally, the impression that this is a "capital-dominated" industry tends to be reinforced by two additional findings. First, man-hour inputs had an essentially horizontal trend, fluctuating between 125 and 150 per cent of the 1904 value in most years, while productive capacity and output increased more than five-fold. Second, output per man-hour varied closely with productive capacity over the long run and with variations in the utilization of capacity in the short run. For details, see [11, p. 71].

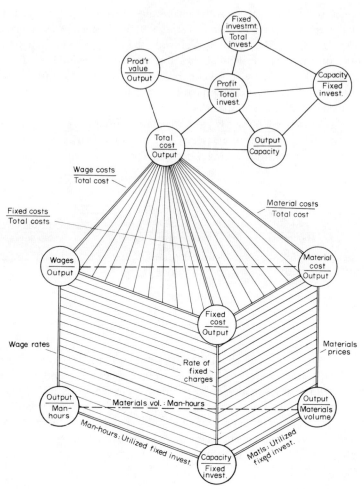

Fig. 2.5. Productivity network, cost structure and managerial control ratios [10].

managerial decisions. And a first step in this direction would involve exploring the cost effects of changes in unit input requirements and factor proportions by superimposing the "structure of costs" onto the "network of productivity relationships" [10] as shown in Fig. 2.5.

The effect of changes in output per man-hour on unit wage costs depends, of course, on concomitant changes in wage rates. Similarly, the effect of changes in unit material requirements on unit material cost depends on accompanying changes in the price of such materials. And the effect of changes in the productivity of fixed investment on the costs of such investment per unit of output depends on the annual rate of charges on such investment as well as on the rate of utilization of capacity. What is being emphasized in this framework, however, is the necessity of considering *interactions* between productivity adjustments and factor prices instead of continuing to make the simplifying assumptions that the latter remain unchanged.

In turn, the effect of a change in unit wage costs on total unit costs depends on the proportion of total costs accounted for by wages as well as on concomitant changes in other unit costs weighted by their respective shares of total costs. For example, if wages account for less than one-fifth of total costs—as is common in U.S. manufacturing [9, pp. 185-91]—a 5 per cent decrease in unit wage costs would tend to reduce total unit costs by only 1 per cent. But total unit costs are more likely to increase than decrease if the innovation engendering the decline in unit wage costs involved increases in unit material and unit capital costs, which together account for more than three times the wage share of total costs in many manufacturing industries[4] [9, pp. 137-42].

Integration of the productivity network and cost structure models thus relates changes in "apparent" input productivities and factor proportions through factor prices to each of the unit costs; and it also relates changes in individual unit costs through cost proportions to total unit costs. Hence it identifies the additional kinds of information required to evaluate the prospective effects on total unit costs of given patterns of past or anticipated changes in the network of productivity relationships.

It should also be recalled that analysis of the effects of productivity adjustments must begin by identifying their sources. Thus, labour-management disputes about the extent of increases in output man-hour and about the proper magnitude of attendant adjustments in wage rates often divert attention from the means and costs of effecting the changes in production processes which account for all or most of the resulting change in output per man-hour.

Finally, managerial decisions in private industry obviously cannot be based on minimizing total unit cost either, in view of the over-riding importance of the rate of profit on investment. Accordingly, the productivity network and the structure of costs must be further integrated with some model of the determinants of changes in profitability, such as the "managerial control ratios" which were presented earlier. According to this system [6, pp. 272-7; 7] it would follow that efforts to increase the rate of profits on total investment need not involve concentration on cost-reducing innovations alone. Indeed, the latter would be deemed undesirable if achieved by means leading to reductions in product prices and capacity utilization levels, which more than offset the prospective gains in profitability derived from unit cost reductions. Conversely, innovations might be deemed attractive if they offer prospects of increases in capacity utilization and in product prices large enough to offset any increases in total unit cost (whether due to higher-priced input factors or heavier input requirements per unit of output).

Figure 2.5 shows how these "managerial-control ratios" may be integrated with the network of "productivity relationships" and with the "structure of cost relationships" to provide a unified framework for systematically exploring the complex of interactions linking changes in factor inputs and factor prices to unit costs and cost proportions and to the other determinants of changes in the rate of profits on investment. This framework may be used in analysing past performance; in developing integrated plans for achieving

---

[4] Change of total unit cost from period 1 to period 2, compared with period 1, is given by

$$\Delta\left(\frac{\text{Total costs}}{\text{Output}}\right)_{2,1} \equiv \left[\Delta\left(\frac{\text{Wage costs}}{\text{Output}}\right)_{2,1}\left(\frac{\text{Wage cost}}{\text{Total cost}}\right)_1\right] + \left[\Delta\left(\frac{\text{Material cost}}{\text{Output}}\right)_{2,1}\left(\frac{\text{Material cost}}{\text{Total cost}}\right)_1\right] + \left[\Delta\left(\frac{\text{Other costs}}{\text{Output}}\right)_{2,1}\left(\frac{\text{Other costs}}{\text{Total costs}}\right)_1\right]$$

specified future targets; or in appraising alternative innovations, even when their initial impacts focus on different parts of the system [9, chaps. 2, 8].

7. Changing Performance Criteria with Increasing Aggregation

Effective management also requires penetration beneath aggregate firm or plant-wide relationships to the behaviour of the component operations which underlie them. Such measures would provide progressively more explicit guides to detecting the loci of all significant changes in input-output relationships and to probing attendant causes and effects over wider sectors of associated operations. Thus, adjustments in aggregate inputs or outputs could be traced to their roots and the effects of localized innovations in mechanization, labour tasks or processing techniques traced upward to aggregate relationships, as will be illustrated later. In addition, productivity measures might be developed whose coverage of activities would conform with established organisational groupings, thus integrating such measures into the structure of administrative controls [9, chap. 8].

It should also be recognized, however, that productivity measures at various levels of aggregation must also fit together into an integrated structure, for component sectors of performance cannot be appraised except in respect to the larger activity matrices from which their tasks have been derived. Thus, improvements in the input-output ratios of one production sector may or may not be desirable depending on its net impact on the rest of the system; and, conversely, managerial efforts to improve productivity ratios for the aggregate system may lower such ratios in some sectors while raising them in others—or lower some ratios in the short run in order to raise them over longer periods.

The relative importance of the various physical, financial and welfare attributes of input and output flows tends to change with the level of aggregation. Within plants and firms, evaluative criteria tend to be derived downward from the guiding objectives of the whole through successively smaller subdivisions; and controls over resource flows tend to be developed backwards from the intended output pattern through successively antecedent stages to initial inputs. Hence, all input-output adjustments must be interpreted within the context of their specified restrictions [8].

Within a component factory producing one part for a marketable product, physical-input-physical-output relationships tend to dominate performance evaluation because the qualitative specifications for labour, materials and equipment as well as their prices and charges are usually set by other units of the organization (e.g. procurement, engineering, industrial relations and accounting). Welfare constraints are also specified for the given unit through health and safety standards, insurance protection and other components of company policies, trade-union agreements and social legislation. Thus, physical criteria are dominant only because financial and welfare conditions are fixed outside the given unit. Indeed, significant changes in any of these prescribed constraints would make it difficult to interpret resultant changes in physical input-output ratios, without careful evaluation of their effects within a larger framework.

In evaluating the larger system which manufactures the complete product, however, cost supersedes physical quantity as the aspect of input flows to be compared with physical output within any given set of physical and welfare constraints. This reflects the production manager's freedom to improve performance not only by decreasing the quantity of each input per unit of output, but also by altering the qualitative specification of inputs, by adjusting factor proportions and by seeking reduced factor prices—all derived from his emphasis on lowering total unit costs. But the interpretation of unit-cost adjustments presents difficulties if accompanied by substantial changes in product design or other constraints.

At the level of the firm, the primary criteria for performance evaluation changes again. Within defined physical and welfare constraints, reducing costs relative to physical output becomes less important than increasing revenue relative to costs; and increasing profit relative to total investment becomes still more important. Thus, one may note a shift in performance measures from (physical input/physical output) to (financial input/physical output) to (financial input/financial output) at these successively higher levels of aggregation within the firm.

In short, because the variety of physical, financial and welfare aspects of input and of output flows may interact with one another, changes in any given aspect cannot readily be interpreted unless other significant aspects remain fixed. Moreover, the relative importance of these different aspects changes not only with the focus of the evaluator, but also with the framework of constraints within which variations reflect performance. With respect to the former, specialized interest groups with distinctive criteria for evaluating input–output adjustments include resource suppliers, resource purchasers (or employers), resource users, product sellers and product buyers.[5]

8. Primary Sources of Productivity Adjustments

Among the vast multiplicity of changes which affect actual industrial operations, eight major types may be selected as having a primary bearing on productivity levels. These are: product design; product composition of output; nature of production processes; scope of fabrication or processing activities encompassed; the effectiveness with which operations are integrated; the productive capacity of operations; the degree of utilization of available capacity; and the nature of the inputs employed.

The categories most likely to account for long term adjustments in productivity levels are: advances in the nature of the processes employed; improvements in the effectiveness with which operations are integrated; increases in the scale of production; advances in the quality of inputs, especially of materials and capital; and changes in the scope of operations. Each of these is capable of engendering major adjustments in productivity levels—advances in integration and in the quality of inputs tending to be individually smaller, but also more continuous, than adjustments in the other categories. Moreover, each of these sources of long-term productivity adjustments tends to raise rather than to lower productivity levels, with the possible exception of adjustments in the scope of operations, which may involve shifts in either direction through "make-or-buy" decisions and those involving backward or forward integration.

The changes in industrial operations which are most likely to account for short-term variations in productivity levels are: changes in the product composition of output; fluctuations in the rate of operations; adjustments in product design; changes in the quality of inputs, especially of labour and of materials; and advances in the effectiveness with which operations are integrated. All but the last of these categories may engender either increases or decreases in productivity levels during short periods. Among these

[5] For a more detailed discussion see [6, pp. 13-56].

categories of change in industrial operations, the greatest adjustments within short periods are likely to be those involving the product composition of output and the rate of operations, although abrupt changes may on occasion affect the quality of labour and material inputs as well. It should also be noted that most of these sources of short-term variations in productivity levels tend to affect the proportions in which factors are combined for the production operations as a whole, rather than altering the nature and efficiency with which individual tasks are performed. Surely, this tends to be true of changes in the product composition of output and in the rate of operations—the most influential of the categories reviewed.

Thus, over the long run, productivity levels may be expected to follow an upward trend, while over the shorter run productivity levels for entire production processes may be expected to fluctuate. It should be emphasized, however, that the latter result is less likely to involve changes in the efficiency with which individual production tasks are performed than changes in the incidence of idleness among the components of operations as a whole, or changes in the product composition of output. Hence, the productivity of actively utilized inputs is more likely to rise than to decline even in the short run, except when extraordinary reductions in the quality of inputs must be absorbed, or when major changes in the product composition of output are experienced by establishments whose product lines differ significantly in respect to their productivity levels or factor proportions.

Of course, actual changes may represent the interaction of adjustments in each of several categories, thus requiring appraisal of simultaneous pressures in various directions. Even more important, it should be recognized that, although these changes affect productivity levels, they may be attended by other effects as well and that these other effects may be either more influential or less influential than the productivity effects from the standpoint of top management objectives. Hence, industrial operations may be changed in directions involving reductions in certain productivity measures, not only because of inescapable market pressures but also because of deliberate managerial efforts to advance other objectives of the enterprise.[6]

9. Constraints on the Utilization of Productivity Adjustments

Two groups of factors tend to narrow the range of alternative allocations of given productivity adjustments: those tending to engender similar limitations in all industries and those tending to produce differing limitations as among industries. The first consists primarily of changes in productive capacity and in physical output; and their effects centre on the choice between expanding productive contributions or contracting the volume of inputs. The second group is rooted in the technological differences among industries; and their effects centre on alternative allocations of the effects of originating productivity adjustments between modifications in factor proportions and changes in the productivity of other direct input factors.

General Effects of Output and Capacity Adjustments

Detailed analysis [6, pp. 182-8] suggests two conclusions concerning the effects of

[6] For a more detailed discussion of the nature and effects of these changes in industrial operations, see [6, pp. 109-24].

changes in output and capacity on factor inputs and factor proportions:
1. changes in output and capacity tend to affect the total volume of inputs by direct production factors rather than the level of effectively utilized inputs of each factor per unit of output; and
2. changes in the relationship of output to capacity tend to affect the proportions in which total inputs are combined rather than the proportions in which effectively utilized inputs are combined.

But it is generally recognized that adjustments in the relationship of output to capacity tend to affect the proportions in which total inputs are combined even without any accompanying innovations in productive processes. Why, then, should special attention be given to the influence of output and capacity adjustments in analysing the effects of productivity changes? First, because changes in the degree of utilization of capacity are an important source of changes in productivity relationships, as was recognized earlier. Second, and of greater immediate relevance, productivity adjustments in themselves give rise to pressures for changing output and capacity, and these changes, in turn, influence the effects of the originating change in productivity relationships. These effects are of only peripheral significance within the framework of physical criteria of productivity adjustments, but they assume more fundamental significance in respect to the cost effects of productivity adjustments.

It should also be emphasized that the effects of changes in output and capacity depend on subsequent adjustments in their levels. This means that the effects of capacity adjustments are likely to be more enduring than the effects of output adjustments and also that the effects of changes in the ratio of output to capacity are likely to be more significant in the short run than over longer periods. Thus, although the general effects of changes in output and capacity on the allocation of the effects of given productivity adjustments within the network of productivity relationships tend to be similar as among industries, the relative likelihood of increases or decreases in capacity may well differ among industries in accordance with their long-term growth patterns, whereas shorter-term adjustments in output are more likely to be similar as among industries in accordance with general cyclical patterns.

Specialized Effects of Production Processes

Attention may be turned now to the second source of constraints on managerial options concerning alternative allocations of the effects of given productivity adjustments: the technological nature of the basic processes involved. And the aspect of the nature of production processes which seems to be of greater significance in the present connection concerns the comparative roles of direct labour, of capital facilities, and of direct materials in determining productive capacity.

Actual industrial processes cover a wide range in respect to the relative influence on productive capacity of changes in direct labour, in capital facilities, and in direct material inputs. One extreme might be characterized as "capital-dominated". This category would include processes in which production workers are engaged overwhelmingly in starting, stopping, loading, unloading, setting controls or otherwise simply facilitating the functioning of machines and other capital facilities. And in this category, materials would play merely the passive role of providing the standardized inputs being acted upon by the machine process. Similarly, the "labour-dominated" extreme would encompass processes in which tools and other capital facilities serve essentially as accessories to wage earners whose manual efforts and related skills represent the fundamental core of the production process—materials once again serving passively as the standardized inputs being acted upon by manual operations. One may likewise envision a "materials-dominated" extreme covering operations in which productive capacity is dominated by the resources to which labour and capital facilities are applied—both of these latter merely facilitating attainment of the production capacity determined by materials and related inputs.

As is generally true of the enormous diversity to be found in the real world, these extremes may well prove to account for but a limited proportion of actual industrial operations. Nevertheless, a summary of the ways in which this classification of processes according to factor dominance tends to affect productivity relationships may shed some further light on the probable effects of productivity adjustments in particular situations.[7]

In operations approximating the machine-dominated extreme (e.g. power plants, cement mills and blast furnaces): increases in labour productivity are more likely to reduce man-hour requirements than to increase productive capacity or the productivity of fixed capital; increases in the productivity of fixed capital are likely to leave direct labour requirements per unit of fixed capital input unchanged or reduced and, hence, to induce parallel increases in physical output per man-hour; and major advances in the productivity of the operation as a whole are thus much more likely to come from—and better measured by—adjustments in the productivity of fixed capital than in the productivity of labour. In operations approximating the labour-dominated extreme (e.g. bricklaying, custom tailoring and carpentry): increases in the productivity of fixed capital are more likely to reduce requirements for such equipment than to increase productive capacity or the productivity of direct labour; increases in labour productivity are likely to leave fixed capital requirements unchanged, and hence to induce parallel increases in the productivity of fixed capital; and major advances in the apparent productivity of the operation as a whole are thus much more likely to come from—and better measured by—adjustments in the productivity of direct labour than in the productivity of fixed capital.

Moreover, both in labour-dominated and in machine-dominated fabricating processes, materials requirements tend to vary with output levels, thus tending to increase the ratio of materials inputs to labour inputs with an increase in the productivity of labour and to increase the ratio of materials inputs to effectively utilized fixed capital inputs with an increase in the productivity of fixed capital. And in such processes, decreases in materials input requirements per unit of output are more likely to reduce the volume of materials input requirements than to increase the productivity of other factors or the productive capacity of the operation as a whole. Also, in both labour-dominated and machine-dominated extractive processes, changes in the richness of materials inputs may be a determinant of significant changes in the productivity of the process as a whole, tending to be reflected by increases in the apparent productivity of both labour and fixed capital.

In operations approximating the materials-dominated extreme (e.g. farming, fishing and smelting), increases either in the productivity of direct labour or in the productivity of fixed capital are more likely to reduce requirements for such inputs than to increase productive capacity or the productivity of materials and related inputs. Also, increases in the productivity of these dominant resources are likely to leave labour and fixed capital

[7] For a detailed discussion, see [6, pp. 188-95].

requirements unchanged, thus inducing parallel increases in the productivity of direct labour and of fixed capital. Finally, major advances in the productivity of the operation as a whole are much more likely to come from—and can be better measured by—adjustments in the productivity of materials and related inputs than in the productivity of direct labour or of fixed capital.

In short, increases in physical output per man-hour are most likely to result from increases in the productive contributions of labour only in labour-dominated processes; in machine-dominated processes, such increases are more likely to be a reflection of gains in the productivity of fixed capital; and in materials-dominated process, such increases are more likely to be a reflection of gains in the productivity of natural resources and related inputs. Similarly, increases in the productivity of fixed capital are most likely to result from increases in the productive contributions of the investment embodied in capital facilities and equipment only in the case of machine-dominated processes; in other processes, such increases are more likely to be a reflection of gains in the productivity of the factor dominating the process. Increases in the productivity of materials and related inputs are in the same way most likely to result from increases in the productivity of these inputs only in materials-dominated processes.

Finally, it is useful to consider briefly how the generalized effects of output and capacity changes differ from the specialized effects of production processes in limiting managerial options in utilizing the effects of given productivity adjustments. In respect to the continuity of their effects through time, it is apparent not only that output tends to vary more in the short run than capacity, but also that capacity levels are more likely to change than the basic nature of productive processes over somewhat longer periods. Accordingly, the influence exerted by initial output and capacity adjustments are likely to be less enduring than those engendered by the basic nature of productive processes. With respect to their susceptibility to managerial control, it is apparent that the basic nature of productive processes is less amenable to managerial manipulation than output and capacity levels. Of course, output and capacity levels must be adjusted to market potentials and competitive forces. Nevertheless, sufficient uncertainty attends such estimates to allow considerable scope for the application of managerial preferences in many industries, especially over an extended period of time. On the other hand, the basic nature of productive processes tends to change but slowly, except under the stimulus of major technological advances, which tend to be uncommon.

The present study concentrates on application of the model which has been presented to successively more complex processes and at successively higher levels of aggregation up to the level of the integrated plant. Some indications of the needed scope of productivity measures for still larger sectors of economic activity including firms, industries and regions are discussed elsewhere [9, pp. 44-48].

10. Hypotheses Concerning Effects of Changes in Productivity and Technology

In order to increase the usefulness of the preceding analytical framework for evaluating the effects of technological innovations, it would be helpful to present a structure of theories concerning probable adjustment patterns under various conditions at each successive stage of interactions. Unfortunately, because of the paucity of past research, few theories are available which can be regarded as reasonably authoritative. It may suggest some analytical foci for other research efforts, therefore, to summarize some of the hypotheses underlying our empirical studies.

In respect to interactions between productivity adjustments and factor prices, two sets of hypotheses may be suggested depending on whether the interactions are triggered by resource-saving innovations or by sharp changes in factor prices. In the former case, it may be hypothesized that the cost reductions expected to result tend to be:

(a) *offset* in the case of labour inputs by rising wage rates, resulting either from piece rates and incentives or from union pressure to reward "productivity gains" (as decreases in man-hour requirements per unit of output are interpreted by labour);

(b) *accentuated* in the case of materials inputs by lower prices due to decreased demand relative to output levels; and

(c) *unaffected* in the case of capital inputs because of the unresponsiveness of interest rates in the vast capital market to reduced demands from small sectors.

Among these responses, wage rates are likely to be the most rapid, inasmuch as local pressures for increases may be expected as soon as a single plant adopts a significant labour-saving innovation. Materials prices, on the other hand, may not respond until the innovation has diffused widely enough to gain recognition of reduced levels of demand. Labour-saving innovations may also tend to spread more rapidly than others because resulting increases in industry wage levels tend to intensify pressures on laggard firms, whereas decreases in materials prices, for example, would tend to ease pressures on firms lagging in the adoption of materials-saving innovations.

When these interactions are triggered instead by sharply rising factor prices—the second form of stimulus—resulting adoptions of resource-saving innovations may merely slow rather than reverse the trend towards rising unit costs, especially during the early years of such diffusion. Moreover, because of the greater uncertainties and other complicating factors involved in the development and diffusion of technological innovations, the response of wage rates and even of materials prices to innovation-induced reductions in unit labour and unit material requirements is likely to be considerably faster than the response of new resource-saving innovations to such factor price increases. And in respect to the latter, rising factor prices may engender faster labour-saving than materials-saving innovational responses in most industries, because general-purpose innovational approaches such as mechanization seem to be more readily applicable to labour inputs than to the replacement of the highly particularistic physical and chemical properties of major types of industrial materials.[8]

Moving further up the integrated analytical framework to cost proportions, it may be of interest to mention certain widely prevailing beliefs concerning changes in these relationships:

(a) that the increasing efficiency of production processes and the more thorough utilization of by-products have led to a progressive and substantial reduction in the ratio of cost of materials to the selling price of manufactured goods;

(b) that sharply increased production per man-hour, attributable largely to more extensive mechanization and more effective management controls, has steadily reduced the relative importance of wage costs in total product costs;

(c) that the proportion of total selling price accounted for by salaries, overhead, and profits has risen significantly as a result of the combined effects of a higher ratio

---

[8] For a more detailed review of these interactions see [11, pp. 118-23].

of managerial and technical personnel to wage earners, of the increased overhead costs attendant on heavier mechanization, and of the maintenance or expansion of profits presumed to have supplied the necessary incentive to further investment in technological improvements;

(d) that, because of frequent fluctuations in raw material prices, in wage rates, in profit margins, and in levels of production, cost proportions in manufacturing are subject to continuous and substantial variation; and

(e) that cost proportions might also be expected to vary randomly through time both because technological advances are assumed to be randomly distributed in terms of their relative bearing on material-saving, labour-saving or capital-saving effects and because managerial choices among them are assumed to be based solely on their prospective contributions to reducing total unit costs.

Working assumptions such as these have had an influential bearing on decision-making in business as well as on broader economic attitudes and expectations. Hence, the development of serious bases for challenging them may have significant implications.

It may be of special interest that our own hypothesis is that cost proportions tend to remain relatively stable over long periods of time.[9] In its support, three sub-hypotheses are offered. First, a rise in the unit cost of one factor as compared with the others—perhaps because resource-saving innovations are relatively less effective in offsetting increases in this factor's price—might encourage shifts in favour of the less costly inputs. Thus, rising unit wage costs due to greater gains in wage rates than in output per man-hour might lead management to increase the level of mechanization. It should be emphasized, however, that the eventual results of such factor shifts might easily be misinterpreted. In this case, shifting part of labour's tasks to machines involving additional capital inputs would have the effect of increasing the "apparent" productivity of labour (as measured by output per man-hour) and reducing unit wage costs accordingly, while reducing the "apparent" productivity of capital (as measured by Capacity/Fixed Investment) and increasing capital charges per unit of output at equivalent levels of production. Such task reallocations help to further confuse *ex-post* efforts to classify innovations as "capital-saving" or as "labour-saving".

Second, progressive reductions in one category of unit costs relative to the others obviously have the effect of decreasing its proportion of total costs and, hence, its relative impact on the total unit costs. But this would tend to reduce the incentive to further reductions in this sector, while increasing the prospective effects on total unit costs of reductions in other costs.

Finally, consideration should be given to the possibility that certain "behavioural" aspects of management decision-making processes may also encourage efforts to counteract developments tending to alter relationships among major cost components. For example, increases in the share of sales absorbed by given cost categories, even when traceable to absolute reductions in other cost categories, are likely to intensify managerial efforts to control costs "which have gotten out of line". Alternatively, increasing specialization may be rendering the maintenance of established proportions among major costs (or functions)

---

[9] For earlier presentations of this view, see [8]. For a negative reaction to the significance of stability in a related sector of economic relationships, see Solow [17]. It should be noted, however, that his analysis was restricted to the wage share of value added for entire groups of industries and even larger economic sectors, thus reflecting the interaction of inter-industry differences both in wage proportions and in cyclical adjustment patterns.

a more practical focus for managerial control efforts than the presumably more funda-mental (but actually more tenuous) estimates of their respective contributions to aggregate performance or net profits. Similarly, the maintenance of past relative budget shares may also represent the most common outcome of efforts to resolve bargaining conflicts among interest groups within the firm in the absence of objective or authoritative determinants.

At the top level of the integrated analytical framework, the relationships encompassed by the managerial control ratios invite still another array of hypotheses bearing on technological innovations. One of these suggests that decisions concerning the adoption of available advances are likely to be as heavily influenced by estimates of the prospective price and output gains offered by attendant improvements in product characteristics as by prospective reductions in the cost of producing them. A more important hypothesis suggests that the progressive diffusion of innovations yielding significant reductions in total unit costs is often likely to engender competitive pressures to reduce prices, thus gradually eroding the initial profitability of such innovations. Commonly used evaluative methods might accordingly be broadened to encompass the dynamics not only of factor price responses to adjustments in unit input requirements, but also of possible product price responses to the progressive diffusion of cost-lowering innovations.

Other hypotheses identify several widely neglected or under-estimated factors tending to reduce below expectations the shorter-term benefits of innovations requiring substantial investments in new facilities. In cases involving the expansion of capacity, it is generally recognized that expected reductions in unit material and unit wage costs tend to be at least partially offset by the increased fixed charges associated with larger investment. But even greater unfavourable effects may result from the frequent under-estimation of: the period required to achieve fully effective functioning of innovative processes; the additional period likely to elapse before attainment of high levels of utilization of the expanded capacity; and the increased marketing costs incurred in seeking to attain the raised sales targets. Moreover, the ratio of Profit to Total Investment also tends to decline during the years immediately following major facilities acquisitions because the attendant addition of undepreciated fixed investment usually exceeds the increment in capacity—especially in cases of facilities modernization—thus lowering the aggregate ratio of Capacity to Fixed Investment [6, pp. 135-45]. Of course, the latter increases in subsequent years as depreciation allowances usually reduce net fixed investment far more rapidly than any concomitant decline in productive capacity.

On the other hand, it may be worth recalling here that the long-term benefits of technological innovations tend to be enhanced beyond the expectations leading to their adoption, partly because of the continuity of technological development efforts and the increasingly effective integration of innovational operations with those surrounding them. Beyond these, experience demonstrates that additional gains in capacity, efficiency and control can usually be obtained merely by easing localized bottlenecks or constraints, rather than adding to the system as a whole. And at least comparable gains may also accrue as interactions with marketing, procurement and transport come to be analysed and improved along with other organizational arrangements.

References

1. American Management Association (1956) *Improved Tools of Management.* New York: American Management Association, Financial Management Series, no. III, 1956.

2. Amey, L. R. (1964) The allocation and utilization of resources. *Operational Research Quarterly*, vol. 15, no. 2, pp. 87-100.
3. Blaug, M. (1967) The productivity of universities. Universities and productivity. Background papers for a conference of the Joint Consultative Committee of Vice Chancellors and the Association of University Teachers, London, 1967, pp. 19-28.
4. *Business Week* (1952) How a big company controls itself. 6 December 1952.
5. Chamberlain, N. W. (1962) *The Firm: Micro-Economic Planning and Action.* McGraw-Hill, New York.
6. Gold, B. (1955) *Foundations of Productivity Analysis.* University of Pittsburgh Press.
7. Gold, B. (1956) New managerial control ratios. *Advanced Management*, vol. 21, no. 4.
8. Gold, B. (1965) Productivity analysis and system coherence. *Operational Research Quarterly*, September, vol. 16, no. 3, pp. 287-308.
9. Gold, B. (1971) *Explorations in Managerial Economics: Productivity, Costs, Technology and Growth.* Macmillan, London. Basic Books, New York.
10. Gold, B. (1974) Technology, productivity and economics. *Omega*, vol. 1, no. 1, pp. 5-24.
11. Gold, B. (1974) Productivity analysis: some new analytical and empirical perspectives. *Business Economics*, May.
12. Horrigan, J. O. (1968) A short history of financial ratio analysis. *The Accounting Review*, vol. 43, no. 2.
13. Jerome, W. T. (1961) *Executive Control.* John Wiley, New York. Chapters 13 and 14.
14. Jones, A. (1973) *The New Inflation.* Penguin Books, London.
15. Kline, C. A. and Hesler, H. H. (1952) The DuPont chart system for appraising operating performance. *National Association of Cost Accountants Bulletin*, U.S.
16. Sanders, B. S. (1962) Some difficulties in measuring inventive activity. In Nelson, R. R. (Ed.) *The Rate and Direction of Inventive Activity: Economic and Social Factors.* Princeton University Press.
17. Solow, R. M. (1958) A skeptical note on the constancy of relative shares. *American Economic Review*, vol. 18, no. 4.
18. Solow, R. M. (1965) Education and economic productivity. In Harris, S. and Levensohn, A. (Eds.) *Educational and Public Policy.* McCutcheon, Berkeley, California.
19. Thorelli, H. B. (1960) Productivity—a tantalizing concept. *Productivity Measurement Review*, no. 22.
20. Weston, J. F. and Bingham, E. F. (1968) *Managerial Finance.* Holt, Rhinehart and Winston, New York. Chapter 4.

CHAPTER 3

Productivity Measurement
– Problems and Methods

BELA GOLD

I. Conceptual Problems of Measurement

1. General Difficulties

Economic measures are obviously necessary for planning, decision-making and performance evaluation in industry and other sectors of the economy. And because necessity
begets responses, a broad array of such measures has emerged into widespread use. So
long as these are employed only for rough descriptive purposes, they can escape sharp
critical scrutiny. But increasing reliance on such data in formulating important company
and industry policies urges careful re-examination of even the most familiar criteria in
respect to their conceptual clarity, the margins within which they are amenable to
measurement and their relevance for the purposes to which they are commonly applied.

Some of the major problems of measuring economic activities for analytical purposes
are rooted in: the nature of the phenomena to be encompassed; the requirements of
rigorous statistical treatment; and the need to interpret resulting data within the context
of the evaluative frameworks of management, investors, trade unions and government
bodies. Difficulties in the first group arise from: the multi-dimensionality of most inputs,
outputs and other elements of economic activities; the tendency for the characteristics of
such economic elements to change through time; the difficulty of measuring some of
these characteristics which seem important; and the inevitable heterogeneity of the limited
number of categories into which the widely differentiated units must be gathered to
facilitate analysis. Such difficulties are intensified by the requirements of statistical
methodology for homogeneity within categories, comparability of data through time,
validity of samples and estimates of the precision of measurements. And any compromises,
shortcomings and omissions involved in coping with the preceding difficulties and requirements must somehow be considered and surmounted before resulting data can be brought
into sufficient conformity with the definitions of economics and related management
sciences to support their utilization in existing analytical models as the basis for interpreting observed findings.

Furthermore, development of an effective system of productivity measurements is
confronted by three additional requirements. First, performance criteria must be designed
to fit the highly differentiated activities found in various subdivisions of complex plants

and firms—and yet such criteria must also be readily amenable to integration at successively more aggregative levels of evaluation. Also, such criteria should permit the appraisal of operations over the wide range of time periods within which activities in different sectors require managerial reviews and decisions. Moreover, alternative sets of measures may be necessary to encompass the distinctive criteria for evaluating productivity adjustments by such specialized interest groups as resource suppliers, resource buyers, resource users, product sellers and product buyers.

Although each of these problems warrants extended examination, it may suffice for present purposes to illustrate some of the less widely recognized difficulties which they present to the evaluation of productivity changes and to review some of the practical expedients for dealing with them within the firm.

2. Output Levels

Managements need to be able to measure changes in the total physical output of their operations for a number of reasons. For example, one cannot assess the implications of increases in total revenue for growth, profitability or effectiveness of marketing efforts without first determining the extent to which the revenue gain was attributable to greater output as over against higher product prices. And similar difficulties are confronted in seeking to appraise changes in total costs unless these can be compared with accompanying variations in total output. Nor can changes in inputs be evaluated without comparing them with total output, or changes in product-mix without reference to total output and attendant rates of utilizing productive capacity.

For such purposes, management requires measures of total output reaching beyond purely physical dimensions—such as the number, weight or volume of various products—so as to aggregate the output of small and large, simple and complex products in terms of their economic significance. Nevertheless, there is still widespread use in major industries of such simple physical measures as tons of steel shipments and kilowatt-hours of electricity generated, despite their obvious failure to encompass the additional costly activities involved: in converting raw steel into a wide range of finished bars, plates, sheets, tubes and strip; or in transmitting and distributing electrical power from generating plants to industrial and residential users.

It should be emphasized that improved measures of the total physical output of multi-product operations have long been available and are widely employed by economists. The most common of these involves weighting the output of each product in the base and in the comparison period by its average price in the two periods.[1] Hence, any change in the resulting total value of all products between the two periods must be attributable to changes in physical output—for the other determinant of total value, product prices, remains identical in the two periods. By thus measuring the relative contributions to output of different products in terms of their relative economic values, or by the cost of all resources absorbed into each plus its overlay of profits, this approach represents an "economically-oriented concept of physical output" [6, pp. 92-97].

Such measures clearly facilitate managerial evaluations of operations by aggregating streams of physically differentiated products into unified total output flows. Among their advantages is that they can accommodate the introduction and growth of new products as

[1] For some purposes, the price weights might be those of the base year or of the comparison year.

well as the decline and elimination of older products. But they are also subject to serious limitations and problems of interpretation. First, resulting measures of output changes may obviously differ substantially from those obtained by using the technological criteria of engineers, or the weight and volume criteria of freight handlers, or the service criteria of consumers. For example, when the average mileage per tyre was doubled by the addition of some chemicals to the rubber, consumers could count each tyre as two in terms of use-expectancy, but production managers could not do the same in terms either of costs absorbed or revenues generated. Second, the use of relative prices as measures of relative physical outputs per unit of product is clearly vulnerable both to the extent that relative profit margins differ among products (as is frequently the case) and to the extent that the ratios of value added to cost of purchased materials differ among products.

Certain other implications of this relative-price-weighted measure of multi-product output may be less apparent. For example, contrary to intuitive expectations, the intro- duction of larger and more complex products need not raise average total costs per unit of output, because the higher cost in the numerator is paralleled by a higher physical output in the denominator (resulting from the greater price weight of such costlier products in computing total output). Even more disconcerting, technological *advances* which lead to lower unit costs and prices for given products also engender *reductions* in the (price) weights given to such product units in computing total output—and *declining* productive efficiency leading to higher costs and prices would tend to *increase* the weights given to such product units in computing total output [7].

But perhaps the most fundamental limitation of such output measures is the assump- tion that each product remains unchanged through time. This may be true for many industries over relatively short periods of time, but the basic thrust of technology is to make this assumption increasingly inapplicable over widening sectors of the economy and especially over longer periods: in manufacturing, in construction and in many sectors of the service industries. As a result, important questions arise in respect to the measurement of changes in prices as well, in view of the already noted critical role of price weights in determining changes in output levels.

3. Input Levels

Comparable problems occur in measuring inputs. One concerns which dimensions of each input category should be measured: what is paid for; or what is used; or the productive contributions derived. Labour inputs, for example, might be measured in terms of numbers employed, man-hours paid for, man-hours worked, energy expended, skills applied, hazards borne and work completed which meets quality standards. Similarly, capital inputs might be measured in terms of investments made, number or volume of equipment and facilities obtained, attendant productive capacity provided, capital charges during a period and actual output attributable to the operation of capital goods. Such choices have to be made partly because some of these dimensions are less amenable to effective measurement than others and partly because given purposes emphasize some dimensions over the remainder. But one must recognize that the various dimensions need not vary in unison and hence that the measurements of one may engender only mis- leading inferences concerning the movement of others.

A second problem of input measurement derives from the fact that aggregation needs and difficulties are usually much greater in this area than in respect to outputs. Even plants of relatively modest size may require varieties of materials and supplies, skill classifications and different types of equipment and facilities, commonly adding up to hundreds of distinguishable input categories. Resulting managerial pressures to combine these into a relatively few key measures of performance have induced resort to various gross expedients. Lacking any meaningful physical common denominator, the variety of capital goods is usually aggregated in terms of *investment values*, i.e. in terms of what was invested on a long-run basis rather than in terms of what was obtained or what is contributed to current productive efforts. The diversity of purchased materials, fuels and other supplies invites aggregation in terms of *current* total *outlays* rather than *physical* units. The latter are still widely used, however, to aggregate labour inputs (although total man-hours disregards wide differences in skills) and also to aggregate salaried inputs (although such total numbers employed lumps together clerks, engineers and executives). Resulting aggregates of major input categories are patently not comparable with one another and their interpretation is likely to be less straightforward than is commonly recognized.

A third problem arises from such internally heterogeneous input categories: how to distinguish changes in the composition of such categories from changes in the aggregate level of any given composition of such inputs. For example, a plant with 1000 wage earners is likely to have more than 200 jobs with significantly differentiated skills. Changes in total man-hours per unit of output are usually interpreted on the assumption that the composition of such inputs was unchanged. Nor is there ordinarily any effective alternative to this assumption inasmuch as the aggregation process tends to ignore the heterogeneous specific input requirements in various sectors of production. This procedure is usually defended, especially over 2- or 3-year periods or less, on the ground that significant changes in the composition of labour inputs tend to occur only over longer periods. It is apparent, however, that the differential flexibility of various labour inputs means that fluctuations in output levels tend to alter the composition of such inputs. Moreover, the tendency for the composition of labour requirements to differ among diverse products suggests that variations in product-mix would also alter the composition of inputs. Thus, this common interpretation is open to serious question even in the short term. In the long run, the changing composition of labour (and of other inputs) is tacitly admitted, yet resulting adjustments in such total inputs per unit of output continue to be interpreted as though alterations in composition were invariably inconsequential.

The errors of under-estimating the effects of changes in the composition of labour (and other inputs) tend to be accentuated by the fact that most plants employ substantial numbers of production specialists who frequently change manual techniques, machine speeds and tooling, and quality standards, which not only define the input requirements for each job, but also affect output norms, basic rates and incentives. Hence, input measurement also faces the problem of disentangling higher wage rates or factor prices for fixed input qualities from the factor price effects of changes in the qualitative characteristics of labour, material or other inputs—a problem already alluded to earlier in respect of output measurement.

4. Product and Factor Prices

Determination of the extent to which changes in the value of production are attributable to output as over against price adjustments depends on clearly distinguishing these from one another. But this is made difficult by technologically-induced changes in the nature of products. For example, if Product A has been modified and sells for a higher price, it may be regarded as essentially the same product (whose units represent the same "amount of output" as before) with an "inflated" price; or as an enlarged (or otherwise improved) version of the same product whose price increase merely reflects a proportionate increase in the "amount of output" (or costs absorbed) per unit of product; or as a new product whose price cannot be compared meaningfully with the past price of a different product. And similar questions arise in respect to input factors, as was noted above. To what extent do higher wage rates, for example, reflect inflationary increases for unchanged labour inputs as over against greater contributions through a shift to higher skills? How much of the increased cost of new equipment and facilities involves paying more for essentially unchanged production potentials as over against obtaining markedly greater contributions?

Efforts to resolve such difficulties are confronted by two conflicting pressures of analytical importance. The pressure for maintaining statistical comparability over time, in the interests of searching out persistent adjustment patterns, encourages under-estimating the significance of changes in the nature of the products and of the input factors constituting the units of measurement. On the other hand, the pressure for increasing the precision of such measures tends to reduce sharply the periods over which statistical comparability can be assured. Resulting data cannot but represent compromises, therefore, involving errors whose significance depends on the purposes for which the measurement is made as well as on the theoretical basis for interpreting the findings.[2]

In economic analysis (and in many accounting reports), the dominant tendency has been to assume that product and factor price changes can be evaluated on the assumption that the products and the input factors have remained unchanged. This assumption is undoubtedly tenable in many cases over short periods, but it is less likely to be true over longer periods for many sectors of manufacturing, construction and services.[3] Thus, the key issue raised concerns the margin of error attributable to this assumption and its implications for evaluating the effects of technological innovations as well as of changes in output and price levels at industry and national levels. For example, before the recent upsurge of inflation, a 6 per cent annual rate of increase in prices aroused widespread alarm about inflation, whereas a 3 per cent rate seemed to be regarded with general equanimity. Yet the question obtrudes itself: within what margins of error are price

---

[2] A recent minor illustration is provided by the controversy in the U.S. over treating the required addition of anti-smog devices to 1971 automobiles as price increases or as quality improvements. A ruling in November 1970 favouring the former was reversed in April 1971, thereby affecting both price and output indexes. The question was characterized by Geoffrey H. Moore, Commissioner of the U.S. Bureau of Labor Statistics, as posing "a complex theoretical issue" (*Wall Street Journal*, 16 April and 3 May 1971).

[3] For example, available indexes of capital goods prices are open to very broad margins of error because of the wide variety and almost continuously changing characteristics of most equipment and capital facilities [14]. Indexes of the price of construction products are also highly vulnerable inasmuch as they are often found to offer indexes of the price of construction input factors rather than of resulting construction outputs [11]. The shortcomings of price and output measures of service industries are, of course, widely acknowledged. Accordingly, recalling the shortcomings of input measurement even in manufacturing industries as noted above, one cannot but be concerned about the emphasis placed by governments on adjustments in "real gross national product" in view of the vulnerability in respect to 60-80 per cent of national output of the "implicit price deflators" used to adjust directly calculated gross national product for price changes.

indexes correct which assume that all or most products and services have remained unaltered, despite enormous technological changes? Such extremely restrictive assumptions also tend to engender under-estimates of the rate of growth of output in terms of attendant service values to consumers. And the deliberate exclusion by such one-sided assumptions of some of the major outcomes of technological advances ensures not only an under-estimation of their effects from the standpoint of conventional criteria, but a decreasing coverage by economic analysis of the forces reshaping the structure and functioning of the economy.

5. *Productivity*

The objectives and requirements of productivity measurement were reviewed in Chapter 2. Oddly enough, one of the most serious problems generated by the development of the "economically-oriented measures of total physical output" mentioned above involves differentiating the results from changes in total inputs (i.e. the sum of all input costs plus profits). Do changes in product value (total costs plus profits) at fixed product prices measure changes in total output or in total input? If the former, as suggested by Fabricant [4], how are changes in total inputs to be measured? Application of the same approach would suggest measuring them in terms of changes in total costs at fixed factor prices, although differing conceptions of profit might suggest their inclusion or exclusion. But what would changes in such total-input–total-output ratios signify? Changes in efficiency levels (as implied by terms like "total factor productivity" [13] and "aggregative efficiency index" [16]; or changes in the ratio of (deflated) total costs to (deflated?) total revenue—i.e. some form of (deflated?) profit margins—or changes in the ratio of factor price to product price indexes?

To answer these questions precisely, one should consider not only the common meanings of the terms forming the numerator and the denominator, but also that changes in these ratios may be due to variations in the quantity or price of each specific input per unit of unchanged product, to differential changes between factor and product prices, to shifts in input factor proportions and to fluctuations in the product composition of total output. The resulting amalgam of interacting effects reaches far beyond the implications of any of the simple interpretations suggested above. Nor can it lend itself to any other interpretation, simple or complex, until an analytical framework is developed which is focused on the relationships among such aggregates within a system having clearly specified objectives. And, incidentally, additional difficulties are encountered when productivity measures developed in the private sector are applied to governmental activities, when measures developed for commodity production are applied to service and construction sectors, and when measures designed to serve the managerial evaluation of operations subject to unified control, as in a plant or firm, are applied to higher levels of aggregation [8]. In short, there is ample reason to re-examine not only the magnitudes reported by empirical studies of productivity, especially at industry and national levels, but their conceptual foundations as well. Moreover, such explorations might usefully be extended to various associated analytical tools as well.

For example, a careful review of the measures underlying the statistics used in estimating parametric values in many empirical studies of production functions raises the question whether results indicate the relative effects on output of equal percentage

45

increments in labour and capital inputs, the prevailing interpretation [15, p. 517], or merely the proportions in which the value of production (or value added) is divided between labour and capital inputs, i.e. cost proportions versus relative factor productivities.[4] Similarly, the usefulness of Leontief's imaginative and powerful tool of input-output analysis may be increasingly undermined by continued acceptance of the view that technological innovations are fully reflected by the technical coefficients within the cells of the matrix, thereby ignoring their often powerful simultaneous effects on shifting the effective boundaries of cells.

Empirical productivity studies can also easily misinterpret the effects of factor substitutions. For example, consider the case when rising unit wage costs due to greater increases in wage rates than in output per man-hour lead to increases in the level of mechanization. Shifting part of labour's tasks to machines involving additional capital inputs tends: (a) to *increase* the "apparent" productivity of labour (i.e. output per man-hour) and to reduce unit wage costs accordingly; and (b) to *decrease* the "apparent" productivity of capital (i.e. output/fixed investment) and to increase capital charges per unit of output at equivalent levels of production.

Lest this discussion be misinterpreted as casting doubt on productivity analysis in general, however, it should be emphasized that major areas of useful application remain. For example, managers of manufacturing operations as well as of construction projects, and even of personal service and government establishments, usually find it quite feasible to appraise input requirements, output flows and performance quality through approximations to the physical, financial and welfare criteria outlined in Chapter 2. Indeed, productivity measurements and evaluations are likely to be open to serious shortcomings only when applied to heterogeneous groupings of activities, or to systems in which the strategic measures of inputs and outputs are not fully known, or to systems which have undergone significant alterations in objectives or activities [9, p. 58].

6. Unit Costs and Real Costs

The original conception of unit cost as the sum of the outlays involved in producing a discrete unit of product is clearly inapplicable in modern large-scale manufacturing operations, which usually involve the simultaneous processing and fabrication of many streams of components which are eventually assembled into a variety of products. Under such conditions, unit costs really represent the average ratio of total costs to total output over a given period rather than an average of the actual costs of each unit of output. At the same time, the increasing importance of indirect inputs—such as planning, control, product development, training and supervision—further complicates the concept of unit costs because of uncertainties concerning the incidence of their contributions as among products and time periods.

But an even more troublesome issue concerns what is meant by the average unit of product which represents the denominator of unit costs. If such costs have been calculated as noted above, the output of plants producing a variety of types, sizes and models of several product lines would, presumably, be expressed in terms of the statistical measure representing an implied "unit of composite product", which is patently non-existent. Suppose, as a simple example, that a plant producing refrigerators of various

[4] For empirical evidence of the enormous difference between these, see [9, pp. 185-91, 195].

sizes and with different combinations of features found that the average production cost per refrigerator had risen by 6 per cent over the preceding year, while the composite average unit had changed from 6.54 to 8.32 in cubic feet of volume, along with some changes in motor design, insulation, freezer space and defrosting arrangements. Clearly, the interpretation of such findings presents continuing difficulties because every change in the "composite product" would undermine unit cost comparisons from period to period as the basis for evaluating plant-wide performance, and because the concept of a composite product is meaningless from the standpoint of production as well as sales [9, pp. 75-81].

In order to help interpret changes in given unit costs (or product prices) over time, these are often deflated (divided) by accompanying changes in the general price level as a means of estimating changes in "real" costs (or prices), i.e. in the quantities of resources absorbed into the products involved. But this technique, too, reflects inadequate recognition of the pervasive effects of technological innovations on the economy. Thus, resource-saving innovations tend to affect factor prices, to spread from their points of origin to other firms and industries using such inputs, and to engender changes in the unit input levels and factor prices of substitute resources. In turn, changes in the general price level represent an average of resulting price changes experienced by a large array of commodities. Deflating the total unit costs of any plant or industry by changes in the general price level can be interpreted most effectively, therefore, as merely indicating the extent to which the given unit costs have changed as compared with accompanying changes in the average cost of resources absorbed (plus profit) per unit of output in the rest of the economy.

It follows that a horizontal trend in deflated unit costs, such as has been found for a variety of industries [7], does not signify an absence of technological progress or an absence of benefits from such progress—as would be implied by the interpretation emphasizing no change in real costs—but simply that such unit costs have moved in unison with the average price of all products. Such a relationship could mean that economies in the plant (or industry) have roughly paralleled those in the economy; or that the industry has withheld the benefits of its differentially greater economies from consumers to be shared by its input factors through higher wage rates, salary levels or profit rates; or that these input factors have received relatively lower payments in order to absorb the burdens of the industry's differentially smaller economies as compared with other industries. Indeed, the deflated total unit costs of any industry could deviate from a horizontal trend over extended periods only if there were a progressively expanding margin (either upward or downward) between its factor prices and profits and those in other industries—a condition likely to be undermined over time by the mobility of resources and by competition from substitute products [7].

7. Capital Inputs

In general, capital inputs may be measured at two stages of their application to production processes. At the first stage, capital inputs consist of liquid funds capable of being expended for a variety of goods and services. This is the form in which they are allocated by suppliers among prospective users. Therefore, both supply and demand are measurable in financial terms. Accordingly, capital suppliers tend to be interested in productivity studies focused on investment fund requirements relative to output levels, thus indicating prospective demands on investment funds for production purposes. Users are also concerned with this measure as indicative of the effect on their capital requirements of prospective adjustments in outputs.

At the second stage of their direct application to production processes, capital inputs take the form primarily of capital goods, including buildings, machinery and tools. It is at this level that physical measures may be relevant. Unfortunately, a review of the various physical measures of capital input which have been suggested does not yield any which is sufficiently homogeneous, precise and relevant to managerial purposes to warrant practical use in decision-making. Those which employ homogeneous criteria (e g. size, weight and horsepower) yield little information about the contribution of the capital goods to production. This identifies the heart of the problem: although capital goods as a whole serve an almost limitless variety of productive purposes, most units have such a narrow range of useful work capabilities that no common denominator has been found for measuring their distinctive physical contributions to production. And it also suggests a workable solution.

As a matter of fact, the user determines his capital goods requirements primarily in terms of the nature and volume of productive capacity required and only as a secondary matter do technical specialists translate this controlling decision into the specific numbers of various types of equipment and facilities to be assembled. Thus, instead of confronting the problem of somehow combining the productive capacity of each of dozens or hundreds of machines and other capital goods, most of which perform highly specialized operations quite unlike those done by others, it would seem thoroughly realistic to measure the productive capacity of the entire installation in terms of the planned level and composition of the output of final products which it is designed to yield [6, pp. 18-30].

8. Productive Capacity and Utilization

In most plants and industries, the level of productive capacity is a basic consideration in production planning, capital goods procurement, production control arrangements, the design of depreciation formulae and in other sectors of plant operations and managerial decision-making. Hence, most managements have in mind, or readily at hand, at least a rough estimate of the productive capacity which they administer. This is particularly likely to be true on a product-by-product basis, if not in terms of a properly weighted composite of all products. It should also be noted that the basic data required for the measurement of productive capacity are usually readily available as the by-product of other plant operation and control functions, including engineering and the establishment of production and cost standards. One may conclude, accordingly, that efforts to develop more precise and more comprehensive estimates of productive capacity are not only feasible in most plants, but would tend to accord with the practical interests of policy-making executives.

In theory, the precise measurement of productive capacity can be made extremely difficult if such efforts seek to encompass all kinds of imaginable but uncommon circumstances. The development of managerially useful estimates of practical capacity, however, involve less formidable difficulties than is commonly supposed. This is especially true under the following conditions:

1. if the measurement is focused on individual plants rather than on the economy at large or on major segments of it;
2. if the measurement is focused on practically sustainable capacity at present rather than on some theoretical maximum under temporary conditions or in the future;
3. if the estimate is made on the assumption that product design and quality, operating processes, and the general character of inputs remain unchanged; that the customary number of shifts and the normally acceptable length of work day and work week are retained; and that appropriate standard allowances are made for breakdowns, repairs and maintenance;
4. if it is assumed that sufficient labour, materials and other inputs are available to service the full utilization of present capital facilities; and
5. if it is assumed that product and factor price adjustments are such as to press for the efficient utilization of all serviceable resources.

Such limitations are readily applicable to a wide range of productive activities. And if complied with, they permit the estimation of practically sustainable productive capacity with but moderate margins of uncertainty.[5] Only in the case of "job shop" plants, producing relatively small quantities of many quite different kinds of products, is the estimation of changes in aggregate productive capacity likely to require specialized studies. Of course, capacity estimates would have to be modified to allow for any deviations from the conditions listed above.

Productive capacity estimates may take two forms: as an estimate of the total amount which can be produced of any given product, assuming some specified allocation of plant facilities to such output; and as an estimate of the composite productive capacity covering some specified mix of products. The latter requires resort to techniques similar to those used in measuring physical output adjustments: essentially involving the combination of productive capacity for each product through the use of relative prices as weights. The results cannot be stated in terms of physical units or in terms of absolute capacity, but only as measures of changes in capacity relative to some specified base year. Such quasi-physical measures, however, may be used to encompass the total output potentials of virtually all plants producing reasonably standardized products whether such product lines are few or many in number. And capacity utilization rates are then determined by comparing the calculated aggregate physical output of a given product-mix with the capacity calculated for that same product-mix, using the same price weights for the output and capacity calculations.

In seeking estimates of sustainable practical capacities for various product-mixes as a basis for planning and evaluating performance, managements would obviously tend to specify realistic operating conditions: omitting marginal facilities; taking account of known bottlenecks; including normal maintenance; and considering only such patterns and rates of production as would accord with current costs and prices. When efforts are made to estimate capacity for entire industries, however, it is usually necessary to resort to expedients which are subject to serious weaknesses[6]—partly because companies may have different conceptions of the uses to be made of such estimates and of the relative advantages of over- and of under-estimates; partly because of the difficulties of aggregating capacities designed to produce at least partially dissimilar products and product-mixes; and

[5] For another view of the problems of measuring productive capacity see Chapter 7.

[6] For a fuller discussion see [9, pp. 44-48 and 10, pp. 14-16].

partly because of reliance on diverse operating assumptions.

Attention should also be drawn to the questionable basis on which changes in capacity utilization are commonly interpreted. Specifically, it is widely held that new capacity tends to be added only as output approaches full capacity utilization; and also that a continuing significant gap between capacity and output implies a serious malfunctioning of the enterprise (or industry). Empirical analysis, however, casts some doubt on both of these deductions. With respect to the former, studies of steel, paper, chemicals and various other industries suggest that increases in output and in capacity tend to parallel one another instead of depicting steplike increments in capacity only as output approaches current capacity limits. Moreover, such studies indicate sustained margins of 20 per cent or more between output and capacity over extended periods in a wide array of industries. These findings emphasize that new capacity tends to be built despite the existence of partly unutilized capacity whenever the new capacity involves the utilization of techno- logical advances, or the manufacture of new products, or closer access either to new markets or to cheaper or better inputs. Hence, the degree of under-utilization often reflects the dynamism of industrial development rather than shortcomings in industrial performance. Under such conditions, the existence of "unutilized capacity" need not signify loss of competitive position or erroneous investment decisions in the past. On the contrary, consistent full utilization over an extended period, far from representing an ideal state, would seem to curtail incentives for responding to new process, product or market opportunities.

9. Fixed Investment

From the standpoint of appraising its role in productivity adjustments, the measure- ment of fixed investment is focused on the current value of the capital facilities and equipment which embody such investment. In common practice, this represents a deduc- tion from the original value of such capital goods in accordance with the estimated wear and obsolescence undergone since their initial acquisition. Such estimates may be made by a variety of means, with consequent differences in results. Moreover, there is no demon- strably correct basis for making such estimates—every procedure being open to significant sources of error both in estimating the pattern of physical deterioration through time and in estimating resultant effects on the value of such goods. If the intention is clear, however, such estimates can be made by the management of each enterprise by whatever means it deems most useful. And so long as a consistent policy is followed in this area, such estimates may be quite adequate for the analysis of changes through time in each firm. It should be noted, however, that some distortions may be introduced into com- parisons covering only a few years or less by the tendency for actual replacement rates to deviate from the steady flows reflected in depreciation allowances, largely as a result of variations in market demand for the user's products, of tax considerations and of efforts to minimize the risks of product and technological obsolescence by recovering investment at a greater than average rate during the early years of equipment use.

Fixed investment represents a concept which is a common focus of business record- keeping, analysis and decision-making. Moreover, the data required for measuring net fixed investment are readily available within any given firm on whatever basis its management considers most desirable—and even in sufficient detail to permit re-computation on alternative bases. And, finally, such data lend themselves to aggregation at industry-wide and still more encompassing levels as well as to inter-firm comparisons, though the latter can be undertaken soundly only over periods of perhaps 5 years or more—so as to allow for variations among them in depreciation practices.[7]

10. Some General Methodological Needs

In addition to the need for extensive re-orientation of the conceptual foundations of some of the basic measures used in the economic analysis of industrial operations, at least brief consideration should be given to three methodological aspects of such measurement: shifting the dimensions of measurement with the changing levels of aggregation representing successively higher levels of responsibility in the managerial hierarchy; adjusting the time periods covered by various measures to those relevant to planning and to evaluating the decisions shaping such outcomes; and exploring the processes of interaction underlying apparent relationships among operating variables.

With respect to the first of these, it should be noted that the relative importance among the various physical, financial and welfare attributes of input and output flows tends to change with the level of aggregation. Within centrally controlled systems (e.g. firms), evaluative criteria tend to be derived downward from the guiding objectives of the whole through successively smaller subdivisions; and controls over resource flows tend to be developed backwards from the intended output pattern through successively antecedent stages to initial inputs. Hence, all input–output adjustments must be interpreted within the context of their specified restrictions (as discussed in Chapter 2).

The second methodological issue concerns the time periods on which various measures should concentrate in order to encompass effectively the results of the decisions and implementation efforts to be appraised. The traditional subdivision of time series into trend, cyclical, seasonal and residual components is subject to serious analytical and practical inadequacies [9, pp. 11-13].

In seeking to measure actual industrial operations, it is necessary to recognize the wide range of time periods within which operating variables are likely to require managerial review and decisions. Production levels and product-mix, for example, may change within periods of a few weeks or less, generating comparably frequent adjustments in labour, materials and shipping requirements. Prices are subject to change within periods of a few months in many areas of manufacturing and even more frequently in retailing. Product specifications, wage rates, salary levels and productivity relationships are likely to change substantially over periods of a year or more. And plant capacity, basic production processes, capital equipment and primary materials are likely to undergo major adjust-

[7] Two additional issues relating to fixed investment have attracted increasing attention. One concerns the need for adjusting fixed investment and associated depreciation charges by some measure of changes in the price of capital goods. Another is the related question of making allowances for improvements in the quality of such goods in evaluating adjustments in their prices. Pressures for adjusting depreciation allowances to changes in capital goods prices tend to intensify during periods of inflation in the interests of preventing the over-statement of profits—and related tax liabilities– due to any inadequacy in the provisions for depreciation reserves needed to maintain capacity despite higher prices for capital goods replacement. Because these questions are only peripherally related to intra-plant and intra-firm assessments of changes in the network of productivity relationships, however, it would be inappropriate in this study to analyse the serious difficulties associated with effective implementation of such proposals. For illustrations of the problems of measuring capital goods relative to their prices, see [2, 11].

ments over still longer periods. Inasmuch as actual industrial operations are invariably the product of a variety of such changes recurring at different rates, economic analysis intended to evaluate different policies and efforts may well require the development of a more flexible array of time-oriented measures more precisely tailored to the specific effects of each of various sectors of decision-making.

A third methodological issue concerns the analysis of inter-relationships. Empirical studies in economics seem to have been dominated in recent years by multiple regression analysis. Despite endlessly repeated *caveats* in statistical theory,[8] the findings are then used either to imply causal sequences with obvious implications for control efforts, or to estimate the effects of changes in the independent variables as the basis for forecasting or planning. But available data series represent only the meagrest array of test borings within the intricate activity systems revealed by our analytical framework. And correlation coefficients do not provide any sound bases for describing the linkages among these test borings, nor for evaluating the relationships between the measured and the unmeasured elements of the system. On the other hand, most managers seem to realize that ostensibly independent variables are strongly or weakly coupled to other components, that some activity sectors are more responsive to changed instructions than others, and that intervening linkages need not adjust automatically to shifts in intended outcomes. Hence, our greater emphasis on uncovering more of the steps and processes whereby given technological advances effect adjustments in certain major aspects of performance than on simply measuring the degree of association between particular parts of the system (whose linkages to one another are not clear and may well change from one setting to another or under different conditions).

II. Measurements and Analytical Methods

Even a brief discussion of the specific methods whereby the preceding concepts can be applied to yield actual measures of productivity adjustments may help to deepen comprehension of the specific changes which are reflected by such measures and those which are not. In addition, the detailing of successive steps in making productivity measurements serves to highlight the options available to management to ensure closer conformity to its own practice and preferences.

1. Output and Capacity Measurement

Inasmuch as value is the product of price and quantity, changes in the total physical output of a multiproduct plant or firm may be defined as the change in its total product value between any two periods not due to changes in its product prices. And the relative change in such physical output may be calculated by multiplying the quantity of each product in each period by its average price in the two periods (or by its actual price in either the base period or the comparison period)[9] and dividing the sum of the resulting price-quantity aggregates in the second period by the sum for the base period. This may

---

[8] For a recent expression of despair about the disregard of such warnings, see Gifford [5].

[9] Use of the average price in the two periods characterizes the Edgeworth index. The others are referred to as the Paasche and Laspeyres indexes. They obviously yield different results when the individual products undergo differential adjustments in price.

be written algebraically as follows:

$$PO_{n,1} = \frac{Q_n(A)\,P(A) + Q_n(B)\,P(B) + \dots}{Q_1(A)\,P(A) + Q_1(B)\,P(B) + \dots} \qquad (3.1)$$

where   1 is the base period and n is the comparison period,
          A and B are different products,
          Q is physical quantity,
          P is the average price.

As was noted earlier, this measure represents an "economically oriented concept of physical output" because it weights the quantity of each product by the economic value commanded by it (or by the cost of the resources absorbed in making it plus the overlay of profits necessary to motivate its production in a market economy). Thus, it reflects any changes both in the quantity and in the price of each product. But it cannot, of course, provide an absolute measure of physical output because there are no common denominators for aggregating units of different physical products.

The basic data required for application of this methodology are limited to the quantity and price (or revenue) for each product in each period—and these are usually available from production and sales records. If prices varied during a period, total revenue may be divided by quantity to yield the average price for the product. Actual calculations may be illustrated as shown in Table 3.1.

Table 3.1. Changes in Physical Output: illustrative data requirements and calculations

Products	Basic Data						Calculated Data			
	Period 1			Period 2				Period 1	Period 2	
	Quantity	Price	Value	Quantity	Price	Value	$P=\frac{P_1+P_2}{2}$	$Q_1 P$	$Q_2 P$	$PO_{2,1}$
A	200	10	2000	150	15	2250	12.5	2500	1875	
B	150	15	2250	100	17	1700	16.0	2400	1600	
C	50	20	1000	75	20	1500	20.0	1000	1500	
Total			5250			5450		5900	4975	$\frac{4975}{5900}$
										$= 84.5\%$

In this illustration, the total value of products rose by more than 3 per cent, but this was due to an even greater rise in the average price of products, leaving a reduction in physical output of more than 15 per cent.

Three questions are commonly encountered in attempting such measurements. The first concerns the extent to which products can be grouped into a limited number of categories instead of differentiating not only various product lines but also the entire array of models and sizes within each. Inasmuch as the computational method can encompass any number of products, management can take advantage of the widest array of product categories with respect to which output and revenue data are available. A second question concerns how to deal with the elimination of old products and the addition of new products. Each can be handled quite simply by the expedient of including only the period in which the product has actually been produced (the earlier period for the older product and the later period for the new product) and weighting it by the price in that period—any attendant errors derived from not using an average price in weighting would tend to be small because the final quantities of the older product and the initial quantities of the newer product would usually account for only a modest proportion of total output (see also Chapter 7).

The third question concerns what allowances should be made for adjustments in the quality of products. As was noted in Chapter 2, if physical conceptions of product quality were to be included in the measurement of physical output—including durability, convenience of use and other attributes of serviceability to consumers—the measure would become unsuitable for the analysis of production operations. The basic point is not that adjustments in product quality are not an essential component of production operations, but rather that a commitment to measure physical output in terms of economic valuations tends inherently to minimize concern with physical and psychological attributes not reflected by market valuations. This still leaves the problem of how to adjust for quality changes involving a significant change in productive contributions as measured by costs and price. One method would be to divide the actual price of the improved product into two components: what would have been the price of the unimproved product if it had shared the average price adjustment of other product categories between the 2 years being compared; and the differential change in price presumably attributable to the differential change in quality. Then the actual quantity of output in the affected category during the second period would be multiplied by the ratio of its actual price to its "would-have-been" price to allow for the fact that each unit of the improved product represents more output than the unimproved 'version. Finally, both this adjusted quantity in the second period and the actual quantity in the first period would be multiplied by the average of the actual price in the first period and the "would-have-been" price in the second, before each was then added in with the price-weighted quantities of the other products in each year.

Another problem which occurs less frequently arises from changes in the scope of a plant's operations involving changes in the ratio of material costs to total costs. For example, a decision to make certain product components instead of buying them would increase intra-plant productive contributions per unit of finished product; yet use of the unchanged finished product prices as weights would ignore this change in the composition of costs. This shortcoming may be minimized by multiplying the quantity of the product after the changed make-or-buy decision by the ratio of the new value added per unit of output (price minus unit material cost) to the original value added per unit.

Like the physical output of multi-product operations, capacity can be measured only in terms of relative magnitudes. One form involves a comparison of capacity with concurrent output to determine utilization rates. Another may be used to measure changes in capacity between two periods. To calculate the first for any given period, one need only specify the product-mix of output, multiply the quantity of each product by its current price and divide the total by the total which results from multiplying the maximum quantity of each product which could be produced under current conditions to yield the specified product-mix by the same current prices. Shifts in the product-mix of output would, of course, require comparable shifts in the product-mix for which capacity would be calculated in order to measure the new utilization rates.

As for the change in total capacity between two periods, the calculation would parallel that for changes in total physical output except that separate comparisons would be necessary for each product-mix. Thus, for any specified product-mix, the maximum quantity of each product which could be produced in each period would be multiplied by its average price in the two periods and the total for the second period would be divided by that for the first to determine the relative change.

Similar calculations might also be used to appraise the prospective effects on economically-weighted measures of total capacity of alternative additional capital investments, especially when these would involve disproportionate increases in the capacity to produce different products.

2. Measurement of Inputs

In order to permit the aggregation of qualitatively different resources, to maintain consistency in input–output comparisons and to ensure relevance to managerial criteria for performance evaluation, inputs, too, must be gauged in terms of economically-oriented (i.e. relative-value-weighted) rather than purely physical measures.

Thus, changes in the aggregate volume of purchased inputs of materials, energy and other supplies can be calculated in the same manner as changes in output. The quantities of each category of material inputs in the base period and in the comparison period are multiplied by the average of the delivered prices paid in the two periods and the sum of such price-quantity products in the comparison period is divided by the sum for the base period, as depicted in equation (3.1); the result measures the relative change in the total cost of materials not due to changes in material prices.

Purely physical measures, such as total wage earners or total man-hours, are not acceptable in the case of labour inputs either. Once again, it is necessary to encompass changes in skill (and attendant relative payment level) categories by weighting the man-hours in each by its relative average payment rates both in the base and in the comparison period to determine the change in the economically-weighted volume of labour inputs between the two periods. Using a table like Table 3.1, the basic data requirements are limited to the quantities of 'man-hours and the total payments (or average payment rates) during the period for each category of labour in the base year and in the comparison year. One can then readily determine the average payment rate over the two periods for each labour category and use these to weight their respective man-hours in order to determine the change in total payments not due to changes in wage rates and hence attributable to changes in the economically-weighted volume of labour inputs.

Several practical issues may be encountered in attempting such measurements. One concerns the treatment of salaried employees closely involved in the production process, such as machine set-up specialists, maintenance staff, inspectors and tool-room personnel. Inasmuch as such categories often result from the further specialization of production tasks, managers seeking to evaluate productivity adjustments in manufacturing operations as a whole might well choose to include such additional categories of inputs weighted by their respective average payment levels. This would seem especially appropriate in the many sectors of industry in which the ratio of salaried to hourly personnel has been rising significantly even within the production organization. A second choice concerns the use of only direct-payment levels as over against the inclusion of various fringe benefits as well, even covering payments to personnel currently laid off. Here, again, management's purpose represents the key basis for choosing. A concern with the total resources absorbed into production would seem to counsel the wider coverage, especially where the expanding array of fringe benefits has significantly increased the ratio of total payments to hours actually worked. And a third question may concern the treatment of overtime. Inclusion of overtime in calculating average payment rates for each labour category would encourage two kinds of confusion: it would lead to a misinterpretation of changes in basic wage rates, even indicating a decrease in such rates after a sharp decrease in overtime work despite an actual rise in basic wage rates; and it would encourage misinterpretation of productivity levels during normal operations. Accordingly, it might be preferable in most cases to treat overtime quantities and payment rates as separate categories from the same categories of labour inputs during normal operating arrangements.

Finally, it should be noted that inventory adjustments have been neglected in the interests of simplifying measurements and analysis. Such omissions could lead to significant errors of evaluation only when inventories are not accounted for on an accrual basis and when such adjustments are both substantial and irregular.[10]

References

1. Amey, L. R. (1964) The allocation and utilization of resources. *Operational Research Quarterly*, vol. 15, no. 2, pp. 87-100.
2. Boylan, M. G. (1975) *Economic Effects of Scale Increases in the Steel Industry.* Praeger, New York.
3. Eilon, S. and Teague, J. (1973) On measures of productivity. *Omega*, vol. 1, no. 5, pp. 565-76.
4. Fabricant, S. (1940) *Output of Manufacturing Industries, 1899-1937.* National Bureau of Economic Research, New York.
5. Gifford, J. K. (1968) Correlationism: a virulent disease in economic science. *Journal of Political Economy*, September.
6. Gold, B. (1955) *Foundations of Productivity Analysis.* University of Pittsburgh Press.
7. Gold, B. (1964) Economic effects of technological innovations. *Management Science*, vol. 11, no. 1, pp. 105-34.
8. Gold, B. (1965) Productivity analysis and system coherence. *Operational Research Quarterly*, vol. 16, no. 3, pp. 287-308.
9. Gold, B. (1971) *Explorations in Managerial Economics: Productivity, Costs, Technology and Growth.* Macmillan, London. Basic Books, New York.
10. Gold, B. (1973) Some frontiers in measuring the economic performance of industry. In DeBandt, J. (Ed.) *L'Information Economique et L'Industrie.* Editions Cujas. Paris.
11. Huettner, D. A. (1974) *Plant Size, Technological Change and Investment Requirements.* Praeger, New York.
12. Jewkes, J., Sawers, D. and Stillerman, R. (1959) *The Sources of Invention.* St. Martin's Press, New York.
13. Kendrick, J. W. (1961) *Productivity Trends in the U.S.* Princeton University Press.
14. Marquard, C. (1960) Costs in the electrical machinery industry. Unpublished M.A. thesis, University of Pittsburgh.
15. Samuelson, P. (1970) *Economics*, 8th edition, McGraw-Hill, New York.
16. Schmookler, J. (1952) The changing efficiency of the American economy. *Review of Economics and Statistics.*

---

[10] For methods of encompassing adjustments in various inventories within the productivity analysis approach developed in Chapter 2, see [9, pp. 155-7].

PART TWO

Applications

CHAPTER 4

A Simple Chemical Process

SAMUEL EILON, BELA GOLD and JUDITH SOESAN

The central objective of the productivity analysis project undertaken by the authors is to improve the measurement and evaluation of productivity changes in industry. In previous chapters a general framework for productivity measurement was developed in some detail, including a review of the literature and a discussion of the concepts and measures most widely used. A number of empirical studies in industry have been undertaken, with the object of testing the analytical framework and its applicability, so that lessons may be learnt when measurement of productivity is attempted in increasingly complex industrial operations.

The present chapter is devoted to the first of these studies, chosen specifically because of its relatively simple process, consisting essentially of a single production stage, with a small number of inputs and outputs. In this way, the problems of data collection and analysis are less likely to be obscured than in the case of a complex process with many flows and several production stages. The study concerns the Newport Plant of BOC (British Oxygen Co. Ltd.), whose major product is tonnage oxygen supplied to the Llanwern Works of the BSC (British Steel Corporation), and the analysis is confined to the period January 1971 to March 1972.

The data collection exercise was designed so as to take account of the structure of relationships in Fig. 2.3, by means of which changes in the underlying network affect total unit costs. At the first level, these involve interactions between changes in the volume of each category of inputs and in the price of that input factor. Resultant relative changes in each unit cost are then weighted by their respective proportions of total cost to determine resulting changes in total unit costs.

By adding the determinants of profitability, as represented by the managerial control ratios in Fig. 2.5, a complete analytical framework is obtained. This provides a systematic approach to tracing the impact of actual or prospective changes in the network of physical productivity relationships on profitability.

The Process and the Plant (BOC Newport Works)

(a) The Process

The Newport plant was constructed in 1963 to fulfil a 15-year contract to supply the

59

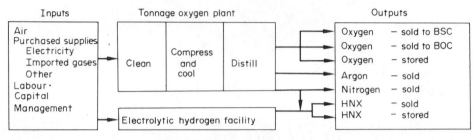

Fig. 4.1. The production process.

tonnage oxygen used in steel-making. Additional contracts cover the supply of a hydrogen–nitrogen mixture, called HNX, used in the finishing process, and also of pipeline nitrogen to a nearby chemical works.

The tonnage oxygen (tonnox) plant consists of three 100-ton-per-day units producing gaseous oxygen, which is piped to the steel works. The process is shown in Fig. 4.1: air is filtered, compressed and cleaned before it enters a distillation column, where the varying temperatures at which the components of air liquefy enable them to be separated and drawn off at different levels in the column (air consists of approximately 79 per cent nitrogen, 20 per cent oxygen and 1 per cent argon). From the tonnox plant, oxygen is normally drawn off in gaseous form, but the facility exists to produce up to about 10 per cent liquid oxygen as well. The latter requires greater compression and hence consumes more electricity.

Liquid oxygen can be stored and then drawn off as a liquid or under pressure as a buffer supply of gaseous oxygen. Nitrogen and argon are also drawn off in gaseous form. The tonnox plants are powered by electricity and supplied with air by a large Demag compressor, which has replaced three AEI compressors, but they are still available for use when necessary.

On the site there is also an electrolytic hydrogen plant, the output of which is combined with nitrogen and supplied to the steel works. Facilities also exist for argon purification and oxygen compression, but these have been omitted from this study.

Thus the major inputs to the tonnox and hydrogen plants, in addition to the capital facilities and equipment, are electricity and labour. The outputs are gaseous and liquid oxygen, gaseous nitrogen, crude argon and HNX. Of these only liquid oxygen and hydrogen can be stored.

(b) The Plant during the Study (January 1971 to March 1972)

During the 15 months covered by this study only three events disturbed the normal running of the plant: in the second week of April 1971 one of Llanwern's two blast furnaces was taken off line to be re-lined. The corresponding reduction in pig iron production resulted in reduced demand for oxygen by the steel-making department. The Demag compressor was not used for some 15 weeks, during which only very small amounts of liquid oxygen could be produced.

Demand from the steel company was again reduced over Christmas 1971, when it shut down for its annual holiday. The Demag was not used for 2 weeks with a corresponding loss of liquid production.

Finally, in the middle of February 1972, demand was considerably reduced as a result of the strike of the National Union of Mineworkers and the consequent loss of power at Llanwern. In this instance the Demag was off for 4 weeks.

During the long period of low demand from April to July 1971 all three plants and the Demag were overhauled; no major repairs were necessary at any time during the period. No significant capital expenditure was undertaken and there were no major changes in policy with regard to plant operation.

Thus, the period under study is characterized by fluctuations in demand from the plant's largest customer; all other parameters governing the operation and performance of the plant remained largely static.

Basic Measurements

(a) General

The measurement required for the analytical framework relies heavily on historic accounting data, which can then be brought together in special ways to permit appropriate evaluations. As discussed in Chapter 3, the output of different products can easily be measured in terms of their values through the use of the Edgeworth formula (by weighting the quantities of each product in both the base year and in the comparison year with its average price in the two periods, as shown in equation (3.1)).

Similarly, on the input side, one cannot measure the total volume of purchased materials and supplies by adding kilowatts of electricity, cubic metres of gases, etc. Nor is this need met by adding their respective costs. Once again, the Edgeworth formula may be used to determine the change in the total cost of materials between any two periods not due to accompanying changes in the price of each component category.

(b) Physical Output

Newport sells oxygen, nitrogen, argon and HNX. The oxygen is sold to BSC, or to the rest of BOC, or it is put into stock. During the period of the study there was a fixed facility charge to BSC for the right to draw oxygen up to a certain amount at a price per hcm (hundred cubic metres) of £0.332 with a second lot (above the prespecified amount) being charged at a substantially lower price per unit. Stocks were valued at about £0.55 per unit and oxygen was sold to the rest of BOC at the internal transfer price of £1.25 per unit. Such differences in price clearly preclude simple addition of quantities of oxygen produced and it is realistic to consider the three categories as three separate products. HNX can be stored and as the stocks are valued approximately twice as highly as sales to BSC,[1] effectively two products are again involved.

Thus, from the standpoint of managerial evaluations the plant produces seven products. These can be combined, using the Edgeworth formula, to compute changes in total output.

(c) Capacity

In the network of productivity relationships, capacity is regarded as the "output" of investment in productive facilities and equipment. No calculations of capacity were made

---

[1] BOC's internal pricing policies have not been questioned in this study.

in the present study because its level remained unchanged over the period covered.

(d) Man-hours

Three grades of workers are employed: plant operatives, skilled maintenance engineers and unskilled maintenance staff (site-workers have been excluded from the analysis because their contributions to the tonnage oxygen and hydrogen plants are indirect and difficult to estimate). Because of their differences in skills and productive contributions, as indicated by their differential pay rates, it would be misleading to measure total labour inputs merely by adding their respective hours; the use of weighting by relative wage rates would be more appropriate.

For example, if 100 hours are worked in grade A at the rate of X per hour and 200 hours in grade B at $3X$ per hour (or three times the A rate), the crude total of undifferentiated hours would be 300, while the weighted total would be $(100 \times 1) + (200 \times 3) = 700$ equivalent hours. If the average levels of skills could be reduced by shifting 50 hours from grade B to grade A, the crude total of undifferentiated hours would remain at 300, but the weighted total would decline to $(150 \times 1) + (150 \times 3) = 600$. This realistically reflects the managerial advantage of a decrease in average skill levels in the form of a reduction in the "equivalent" hours of labour input.

Accordingly, wage rates and hours-worked data were collected for each grade as the basis for calculating the total of weighted man-hours of labour input.

(e) Materials Volume

The three major categories of purchased materials and supplies are: electricity, which averages more than 60 per cent, imported gases, and other purchased supplies.[2] Both liquid nitrogen and liquid oxygen are imported for storage. The former is not produced at all in Newport and hence is a regular import, while liquid oxygen has to be imported only in cases of relative emergency. When demand from the steel works is significantly lowered, power can be saved by turning off one of the three tonnox plants. Because the large Demag compressor cannot be turned down to any large extent, its closure must be replaced by two of the AEI compressors. But these do not compress sufficient air to allow liquid oxygen production, necessitating at such times imports of liquid oxygen. Hydrogen is regarded as an import to the tonnox plant from the hydrogen plant. Application of the Edgeworth formula to calculate changes in the volume of materials inputs follows equation (3.1) and the example in Table 3.1 in Chapter 3.

(f) Factor Prices

Factor prices are the intermediate link between changes in input quantities per unit of output and changes in the unit cost of such inputs, as shown in Fig. 2.5. Accordingly,

[2] The "other purchased supplies" component of materials inputs includes such miscellaneous items as caustic soda, engineering supplies, valves, payments to Head Office for annual overhauls and "other purchased materials". No meaningful physical quantities were available to relate to the money spent on these items. It seemed likely that over so short a period prices of the items would not have changed drastically and it was therefore assumed that they had not changed at all, so that the value could also represent a volume measure. (Over a longer period, it would have been necessary to explore actual changes in the rates paid for at least the larger items within this category in order to estimate possible volume changes more closely.)

A SIMPLE CHEMICAL PROCESS

Table 4.1. Indexes of Output, Inputs and Input–Output Relationships

Date	Output	Capacity	Direct inputs			Apparent input productivities			Factor proportions		
			Materials volume	Man-hours	Net fixed investment	Output Mat. vol.	Output Man-hr	Capacity Fixed inv.	Mat. vol. Man-hr	AUI_F† Mat. vol.	AUI_F† Man-hr
1/71	100.0	100.0	100.0	100.0	100.0	100.0	100.0	100.0	100.0	100.0	100.0
2/71	101.6	100.0	99.7	101.1	99.0	101.9	100.5	101.1	98.6	100.8	99.4
3/71	101.3	100.0	107.4	103.1	97.9	99.9	98.3	102.1	98.3	97.8	96.2
4/71	83.8	100.0	79.6	106.4	96.9	105.3	78.8	103.2	74.8	102.0	76.3
5/71	77.9	100.0	80.8	108.8	95.8	96.4	71.6	104.4	74.3	92.3	68.6
6/71	74.8	100.0	73.7	99.1	94.8	101.5	75.5	105.5	74.3	96.2	71.5
7/71	83.2	100.0	98.2	101.4	93.7	84.7	82.1	106.7	96.8	79.4	76.9
8/71	95.9	100.0	106.4	92.3	92.7	90.1	103.9	107.9	115.3	83.6	96.3
9/71	98.9	100.0	97.5	97.9	91.7	101.4	101.0	109.1	99.6	92.9	92.5
10/71	98.4	100.0	105.5	98.6	90.6	93.3	99.8	110.4	107.0	84.5	90.5
11/71	96.4	100.0	102.0	103.0	89.6	94.5	93.6	111.7	99.0	84.6	83.8
12/71	89.5	100.0	90.3	95.0	88.5	99.1	94.2	113.0	95.1	87.7	83.4
1/72	96.2	100.0	106.7	99.2	87.5	90.2	97.0	114.3	107.6	78.8	84.8
2/72	87.1	100.0	82.5	99.3	86.4	105.6	87.7	115.7	83.1	91.3	75.8
3/72	99.6	100.0	100.9	96.8	85.4	98.7	102.9	117.1	104.2	84.2	87.8

† AUI_F: Actively Utilized Fixed Investment (Fixed Investment $\times \frac{\text{Output}}{\text{Capacity}}$).

one may either collect factor price data for each input directly or calculate them by dividing any change in the total cost per unit of output for each input category by accompanying changes in its quantity per unit of output.

In this study the latter approach was adopted, because of the availability of data for total costs and total input quantities for each category—thus yielding measures of any changes in the average price of each input factor. It was simpler in all cases to collect data on total costs for each category of input and to work backwards to the implied rate. For example, the materials price index (M_P) could be determined by first obtaining total materials costs (M) and employing the identity $M \div M_V = M_P$ where M_V denotes the materials volume and M_P the price. The exercise was simplified by the fact that the price of electricity (the major material input) did not change during the period under consideration.

(g) Financial Data

Net fixed investment is of concern in productivity analysis because it indicates the volume of capital funds still tied up in facilities and equipment which management seeks to utilize so as to yield required rates of return. Inasmuch as all facilities and equipment in the Newport plant are depreciated on a straight-line basis over a 15-year period and no new investments were made during the period studied, net fixed investment simply declined steadily, as shown in Table 4.1.

In general, few problems are likely to be encountered in seeking data on turnover, total costs, profits and investment because accounting systems usually provide for the regular determination of such information. In the case of the Newport plant, a minor problem was provided by the fact that "working capital" was not a meaningful concept to such a small part of a large decentralized organization. For the sake of completeness, an arbitrary figure was taken (sufficient to cover 3 months costs), although its inclusion had an insignificant effect on the final results. This was then added to net fixed investment to calculate total investment.

Data-Collection Experience

(a) General

Data were collected for the 15 months between January 1971 and March 1972, which involved no significant changes in plant facilities, accounting practices, wage rates, electricity rates or in the basic price of oxygen to the British Steel Corporation. Such possible complications were avoided for the same reason that a relatively simple production process was chosen: to permit initial concentration on the application aspects of the model and on measuring inputs and outputs to fit the operating practices and records available in the plant.

Most of the data required were indeed readily available and were collected in little more than three man-days because of the analytical model's conformity with BOC's accounting practices. Actual sources used included: production schedules, sales invoices, profitability assessments and manpower statistics. Monthly data had to be adjusted for the coverage of 5 weeks every third month.

(b) Special Problem in Measuring Output

Tonnage oxygen supplied to the BSC is the cheapest product sold, but by its volume it dominates total output none the less. When its average monthly price was calculated by the usual procedure of dividing the total revenue from its sales by the quantity supplied, the results fluctuated so widely—from 69p to 102p per hcm—that it clearly misrepresented the existence of a fixed price schedule. This led to a detailed examination of the sales contract which revealed that BSC must pay a fixed facility charge of nearly £10,000 per week merely for *the right to draw* up to 31,000 hcm of oxygen per week at £0.33 per hcm for the first 25,000 hcm and £0.12 per hcm thereafter. Thus, they pay a type of rent for the facilities provided plus a constant rate for every unit consumed. During periods of very low oxygen consumption, therefore, the price per unit rose sharply, because the entire facility charge was allocated over the limited consumption—although neither the basic facility charge nor the additional price per unit varied during the period studied. This problem was overcome by treating the facility charge as payment for a separate product, i.e. oxygen-supply facilities, of which a constant amount was bought each month. Actual oxygen consumption was then priced in accordance with the amounts consumed at each of the two applicable rates.

Results and Analysis

The data collected and the results are summarized in the following tables and figures. As was envisaged at the outset of the study, the results follow expected economic trends in the main and, where they appear unusual, explanations are readily available related to events in the period in question.

(a) Outputs and Inputs

Figure 4.2 shows that physical output for the major products remained fairly steady

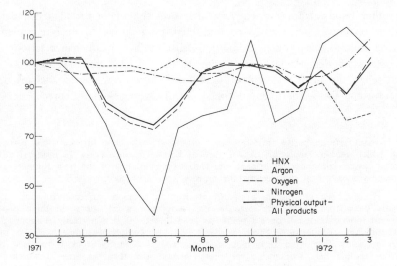

Fig. 4.2. Index of physical output and its components.

65

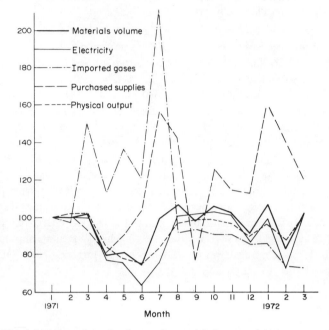

Fig. 4.3. Index of total volume of materials input and its components.

throughout the period, apart from the 4 months of April to July 1971 (the fall in production being due to a fall in demand from BSC).[3]

Figure 4.3 shows the major part played by electricity in determining the size of total materials volume. A fairly steady trend is interrupted again by a slump over the same period, reflecting the essentially variable nature of electricity usage. The very high level of imported gases during the same period is interesting despite its less significant impact on materials volume.[4]

As for other inputs, labour varied very little over the whole period, particularly in the case of plant operatives. Only three or four men are required to operate a plant and no fewer can be utilized, even when production falls. In fact, maintenance labour showed a slight increase when demand was low, owing to the fact that maintenance work could be carried out when the plant was not fully utilized. Capacity remained unchanged throughout the period and fixed investment declined linearly with assumed depreciation.

[3] Steel is manufactured partly from pig iron produced in a blast furnace. Blast furnaces have a brick lining which requires replacing (in the case of Llanwern, once every 18 months) during which time the blast furnace produces no iron at all. The re-lining of one of the blast furnaces explains the lack of demand for oxygen at the steel-making process from April to July 1971.

[4] As has already been mentioned, a significant drop in demand can result in one of the three tonnox plants being turned off. The large Demag compressor which serves all three plants can be turned down to some extent, but once a plant has been turned off it is normally economical to switch to two of the AEI compressors. These, however, do not compress sufficient air to provide the refrigeration necessary for liquid oxygen production, and if a buffer stock is required it must be imported from another BOC works at a very much higher price than the price at which it could be produced. Thus, the high values for imported gases during the 4-month period of low demand relate to this liquid oxygen.

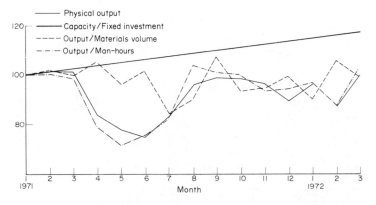

Fig. 4.4. Physical output and apparent productivity of direct inputs.

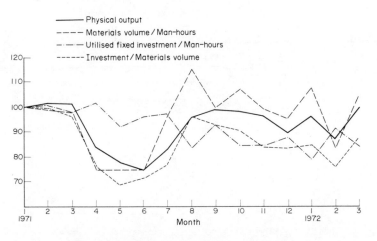

Fig. 4.5. Physical output and factor proportions.

(b) Productivity and Costs

Figure 4.4 shows how the productivity of materials remained fairly steady, despite changes in output (since a significant part of materials consists of electricity, which varies with output, this is to be expected). However, output per man-hour is seen to vary with output, reflecting the fact that labour is largely fixed. Materials and actively utilized fixed investment fall in relation to labour when output falls, as shown in Fig. 4.5. Thus, in all cases, the factor inputs and factor proportions follow expected trends, given the nature of the industry and the history of demand during the period under study.

Figure 4.6 shows how wages and capital unit costs increase as output falls; total unit costs also increase, although material costs (the variable element) remained relatively constant throughout the period. Cost proportions, shown in Fig. 4.7, remained steady, apart from a slight fall in material costs during the low-demand interval. In general, wages account for about 5 per cent of total costs, materials about 60 per cent, depreciation about 20 per cent and other costs about 15 per cent.

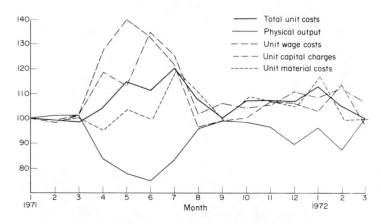

Fig. 4.6. Total unit costs and its components.

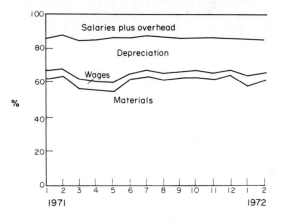

Fig. 4.7. Cost proportions.

(c) Managerial Control Ratios

Profit per unit of output, shown in Fig. 4.8, follows roughly the same trend as output, as one would expect from the pricing policy for tonnage oxygen at Newport (although a lower price per unit is charged beyond a given demand level, it more than covers the marginal input costs at that production volume). Other managerial control ratios are shown in Fig. 4.9.

One interesting, and somewhat unexpected, result was the dramatic increase in unit profit during the last month of the period. Output for that month was approximately at an average level, and yet the total revenue was higher than average. This appears to be due to two factors: exports of oxygen were double the corresponding level during the base period, while argon had not only doubled in volume but its price rose by some 44 per cent. This analysis suggests that oxygen exports and argon sales are extremely profitable, even though they appear to have little effect on the total plant output.

68

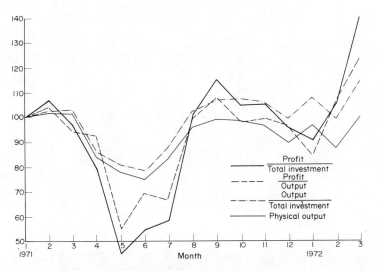

Fig. 4.8. Managerial control ratios and output

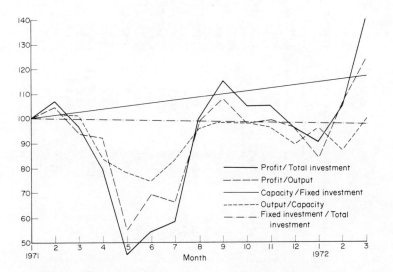

Fig. 4.9. Additional managerial control ratios.

Use of the Model

The prime use of the model described above is to analyse the effects of changes in any of the components of the model at whatever level (including changes in factor productivities, proportions or prices) on the other components and on the total cost. In particular, changes in quantities and prices of input and output factors can be systematically evaluated. For example, it is possible to ask such questions as: what would be the effect of

a 10 per cent reduction in the quantity of labour required?

69

Table 4.2. Cost Proportions and Indexes of Factor Prices and Unit Costs (January 1971 = 100)

Period	Factor prices			Unit costs					Cost proportions			
	Average wage rate	Average material prices	Rate of charges on fixed int.	Unit wage cost	Unit material cost	Unit fixed inv. charges	Other unit costs	Total unit costs	Wages %	Materials %	Deprecia- tion %	Other costs %
1/71	100.0	100.0	100.0	100.0	100.0	100.0	100.0	100.0	4.7	61.7	19.9	13.7
2/71	99.9	100.5	101.1	99.4	98.6	98.4	102.0	99.0	4.7	61.4	19.8	14.1
3/71	99.9	99.7	105.0	101.6	99.7	101.5	89.2	98.5	4.8	62.5	20.3	12.4
4/71	99.9	100.1	102.6	126.8	95.1	118.6	118.6	104.2	5.7	56.3	22.5	15.5
5/71	99.9	100.1	108.2	139.5	103.9	113.1	131.8	114.9	5.7	55.8	22.9	15.6
6/71	100.0	100.1	106.2	132.5	98.7	134.6	129.8	111.4	5.5	54.7	23.9	14.1
7/71	100.0	100.0	112.0	121.8	118.0	126.1	124.9	120.6	4.7	60.5	20.7	14.1
8/71	99.9	100.0	105.2	96.2	110.9	101.7	106.3	107.6	4.2	63.7	18.7	13.4
9/71	100.0	100.1	114.5	99.0	98.7	106.2	100.5	100.2	4.6	60.8	20.9	13.7
10/71	100.0	101.4	113.3	100.2	108.7	104.3	108.9	107.2	4.4	62.6	19.2	13.8
11/71	100.0	101.6	113.5	106.8	107.4	105.3	110.3	107.2	4.6	61.9	19.4	14.1
12/71	99.9	104.1	111.8	106.1	105.1	110.5	111.8	106.9	4.6	60.7	20.4	14.3
1/72	99.9	104.1	119.1	103.0	115.4	108.4	112.3	112.7	4.3	63.2	18.9	13.6
2/72	100.0	104.1	113.0	114.0	98.6	112.1	120.4	104.8	5.1	58.1	21.1	15.7
3/72	99.9	97.3	118.3	97.1	98.5	101.4	106.2	99.8	4.5	60.9	20.0	14.6

a 10 per cent increase in the price of raw materials?

diverting 10 per cent of resources from one product to another?

a 10 per cent fall in the price of a given product?

Such questions can be answered by tracing the effect of the change from its source through each component and level in the system, until finally the overall effect on profitability is ascertained.

The following example (based on the data in Tables 4.1-4.3) illustrates this use of the model. Suppose that the following forecasts were made in January 1971 for a given future period:

a 10 per cent increase in the demand for gaseous oxygen from the BSC,

a 5 per cent increase in the wage rate for all grades of labour,

a 10 per cent increase in the price of electricity.

(For the purposes of this illustration, the automatic link between electricity prices or wages and the price of oxygen specified in the sales contract between BOC and BSC will be ignored.) It is further assumed that a 10 per cent increase in the output of oxygen will only necessitate a 5 per cent increase in the consumption of electricity and no increase in labour requirements. The following questions may now be posed:

(a) What will be the effects of these changes on the productivity, cost structure and profitability of the plant?

(b) To what extent must the unit price of the second lot of oxygen supplied to the BSC be changed to maintain profitability at its existing level (without changing the facility charge and the price for the first lot)?

Table 4.4 shows the results of computations based on the model. The second column shows that the volume of materials is expected to rise, because of increased consumption of electricity. Output too will rise, but by considerably less than the 10 per cent increase in the demand for gaseous oxygen by BSC (this is because of the very low price weight attributed to this oxygen in the Edgeworth formula for total output). Thus, the productivity of materials is expected to fall, while that of labour would rise, since relatively more materials than labour would be used. Total unit costs would be expected to rise by 6.4 per cent, so that without any increase in prices this would result in a fall in absolute profits and thus in profit per unit. The expected fall in return on investment (Z/I_F) of

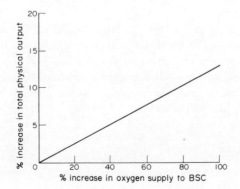

Fig. 4.10. Percentage rise in total physical output.

71

Table 4.3.

Indexes of Managerial Control Ratios and their Components (January 1971 = 100)

Revenue, investment and profits

Period	Revenue	Total costs	Profits	Net fixed inv.	Working capital	Total inv.
1/71	100.0	100.0	100.0	100.0	100.0	100.0
2/71	102.3	100.6	105.9	99.0	100.0	99.1
3/71	98.4	99.8	95.2	97.9	100.0	98.2
4/71	84.2	87.3	77.3	96.9	100.0	97.3
5/71	74.6	89.5	42.8	95.8	100.0	96.4
6/71	73.3	83.3	51.9	94.8	100.0	95.5
7/71	86.0	100.3	55.3	93.7	100.0	94.6
8/71	100.3	103.2	94.1	92.7	100.0	93.7
9/71	101.6	99.1	106.7	91.7	100.0	92.8
10/71	102.6	105.5	96.2	90.6	100.0	91.9
11/71	100.8	103.3	95.5	89.6	100.0	91.0
12/71	92.7	95.7	86.2	88.5	100.0	90.1
1/72	99.6	108.4	80.6	87.5	100.0	89.2
2/72	91.7	91.3	92.7	86.4	100.0	88.3
3/72	107.0	99.4	123.3	85.4	100.0	87.4

11.6 per cent would be due to the fall in profit per unit of output (Z/PO) of 12.7 per cent offset by the increase in capacity utilization (PO/CAP) of 1.3 per cent.[5]

The third column shows that in order to maintain profit per unit at the existing level the price of the last units of gaseous oxygen must be increased by 70 per cent. Such increase in price would still have a relatively small effect on the measure of output and on productivity and factor proportions as shown, but the increase in revenue is sufficient to offset the increases in production costs. It should also be noted that in this case the average price per unit (calculated as the sum of the fixed facility charge, the price paid for the first lot of oxygen supplied and the price for the second lot divided by the total demand) would in fact decline from 0.689 to 0.649, in spite of the proposed increase in the unit price charged for the second lot (the reason for this is that the facility charge and the amount of the first lot, as well as its price, remain unchanged, while the increase of total demand is assigned to the second lot and is sufficiently large to offset the increase in its marginal price).

Thus the model can be used not only to trace the effects of expected changes in any of its parameters, but also to estimate the responses needed on the part of management in order to maintain or achieve desirable levels of profitability.

The model also serves to draw attention to important relationships between various parameters within the plant. One result of particular interest in this example is the insensitivity of total output to changes in the output of oxygen for the BSC (all other output components being equal). Figure 4.10 further illustrates the fact that each 10 per cent increase in the output of oxygen for the BSC raises total output by only 1.3 per cent. This finding corroborates an earlier conclusion that significant changes in profitability are likely to be effected via oxygen for export or argon, rather than by the primary product of the plant, namely tonnage oxygen.

[5] See further details in Chapter 7.

Table 4.3. (cont.)

Managerial control ratios

Revenue Output	Costs Output	Output Capacity	Capacity Net fix.inv.	Net fix.inv. Tot. inv.	Profit Tot. inv.	Profit Output	Output Tot. inv.
100.0	100.0	100.0	100.0	100.0	100.0	100.0	100.0
100.7	99.0	101.6	101.1	99.9	106.8	104.2	102.5
97.1	98.5	101.3	102.1	99.7	96.9	94.0	103.2
100.5	104.2	83.8	103.2	99.6	79.4	92.2	86.1
95.8	114.9	77.9	104.4	99.4	44.4	54.9	80.8
98.0	111.4	74.8	105.5	99.3	54.3	69.4	78.3
103.4	120.6	83.2	106.7	99.1	58.4	66.5	87.9
104.6	107.6	95.9	107.9	98.9	100.5	98.1	102.3
102.7	100.2	98.9	109.1	98.8	115.0	107.9	106.6
104.3	107.2	98.4	110.4	98.6	104.7	97.8	107.1
104.6	107.2	96.4	111.7	98.4	105.0	99.1	105.9
103.6	106.8	89.5	113.0	89.3	95.7	96.3	99.3
103.5	112.7	96.2	114.3	98.1	90.4	83.8	107.8
105.3	104.8	87.1	115.7	97.9	104.9	106.4	98.6
107.4	99.8	99.6	117.1	97.7	141.1	123.8	114.0

Conclusions

The analysis in this chapter illustrates three important attributes of the model introduced in Chapter 2. The value of each will naturally depend on the nature of the plant, on the constraints imposed upon it and on the ability of management to question the constraints and to institute possible changes.

The first attribute is that the model provides a systematic process for data collection and analysis that is bound to improve the user's understanding of the plant and the interrelationships between the major parameters at play. It can help to tighten definitions of inputs, outputs and costs. It can be used to ascertain what level of aggregation of inputs and/or outputs is most appropriate for the plant in question.

Secondly, the model can be used for recording productivity ratios, factor and cost proportions over time, so that when significant changes occur their causes can be traced back through the model. The figures illustrate how such historical records can be analysed; where certain trends can be established, or where particular factors are found to be predominant, management may be forewarned about undesirable events and may wish to examine possible courses of action.

Thirdly, the model can be used to anticipate future results. The effects of changes in exogenous variables, as well as in those parameters which the manager can influence, are important for the decision-making process, and can improve his ability to forecast and assess the outcome of various arrays of possible events. The example quoted earlier illustrates these points: it showed what would happen if certain changes occur outside the manager's control (such as the level of demand and the cost of materials) and what action would be required of him to adjust the price (assuming it is possible) to offset their adverse effect on profitability.

This example refers to the expected outcome corresponding to various components in the system, based on single value estimates of others stated in the form of deterministic

Table 4.4. Effects of Change for a Given Example

	January 1971	Expected result (a) (no change in oxygen price)	Expected result (b) (oxygen price up 70%)
Physical inputs			
Materials volume (M_V)	100	104	104
Man-hours (M-hr)	100	100	100
Fixed investment (I_F)	100	100†	100†
Physical outputs			
Output (PO)	100	101.3	103.6
Capacity (CAP)	100	100	100
Productivities			
PO/M_V	100	97.4	99.6
PO/M-hr	100	101.3	103.6
CAP/I_F	100	100†	100†
Factor proportions			
M_V/M-hr	100	104	104
AUI_F/M_V	100	97.4	99.6
AUI_F/M-hr	100	101.3	103.6
Unit costs			
W/PO (wages)	100	103.7	101.4
M/PO (materials)	100	110.9	108.4
CC/PO (capital charges)	100	98.7	96.5
Others/PO (other expenses)	100	98.7	96.5
TC/PO (total unit costs)	100	106.4	104.1
Cost proportions			
W/TC (wages)	100	96.5	96.5
M/TC (materials)	100	104.2	104.2
CC/TC (capital charges)	100	92.9	92.9
Others/TC (other expenses)	100	92.5	92.5
Managerial control ratios			
Profit (Z)	100	88.4	100
Unit profit (Z/PO)	100	87.3	96.5
Return on fixed investment (Z/I_F)	100	88.4	100

† These data would change over time as a result of the depreciation of fixed investment. In this example changes due to time are ignored so as to highlight the effects of the forecast changes in demand and factor prices.

forecasts. A more sophisticated approach would require these forecasts to be expressed as ranges of values, or as distributions, so that samples from the ranges or distributions would have to be taken in tracing their effects through the model. This "risk simulation" approach would allow the possible effects to be described in distribution-form and could provide a means of performing a sensitivity analysis on the model in general and for specific forecasts in particular. The application of this method is further discussed in Chapter 8.

Thus, the model can become a useful part of the planning process. It can help determine pricing policies and product-mix, as well as provide valuable information in negotiations on wages and cost of materials.

CHAPTER 5

Complex Steel Processes

BELA GOLD and JUDITH SOESAN

The preceding analysis of a single process plant was followed by a series of studies of the complex interwoven processes of the Port Talbot Works of the British Steel Corporation. As the result of a succession of major post-war development programmes terminating just prior to the beginning of the period covered by our studies, this had become one of the largest integrated iron and steel plants in Europe with a steel-making capacity of 3.25 million tons per year.

In addition to the general analytical and managerial purposes of the studies which were summarized at the outset, the following intensive probing of component operations had two methodological aims: to test the applicability of the original productivity network and cost structure framework to more variegated arrays of inputs, more intricate production flows and wider arrays of product categories; and to make a practical determination of the availability of the kinds of data required for such analysis on the basis of the kinds of manning, production control and accounting information already being collected for established managerial purposes.

A simplified flow chart of the major operations involved is shown in Fig. 5.1. Coal is fed into coke ovens to produce coke, coke gas and coke breeze. Most of the coke is charged into blast furnaces along with ore and limestone to produce molten pig iron. All of the latter is fed into steel furnaces together with scrap steel and oxygen to yield steel ingots, most of which are rough rolled in the slab mill. Subsequent processing stages produce a variety of hot and cold rolled as well as coated steel products.

The following analysis focuses successively on the three operating departments into which the plant is divided—iron-making, steel-making and finishing—before examining the performance of the plant as an integrated whole. This chapter summarizes the results of the departmental studies and the next chapter considers the plant findings. In each case, an 8-year period from September 1964 to March 1972 will be covered.[1]

The framework for collecting data was derived from the models in Chapter 2 (Figs. 2.3 and 2.5) which require information about:

output and capacity;

inputs of labour, materials and fixed investment; and

---

[1] The changeover to 31 March as the end of the financial year in 1970 resulted in a "6-month year" for 1969/70, and the data were therefore correspondingly weighted in the calculations for that "year".

factor prices, including wage rates, materials prices and capital charge rates.

These data then made possible the calculation of indexes of changes in each of the following components of the network of productivity relationships and its superstructure of cost relationships:

direct input productivities: labour; materials; and net fixed investment;

direct input proportions: labour/materials; labour/utilized capital; and materials/utilized capital;

unit production costs: wages; materials; capital charges; and other costs;

cost proportions: wages/total costs; materials/total costs; capital charges/total costs; and other costs/total costs;

total unit production costs.

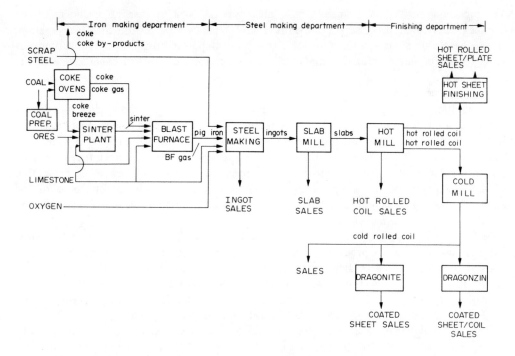

Fig. 5.1. Simplified flowchart of operations at Port Talbot steelworks.

I. Iron-making

The iron-making department's major components are the coal preparation plant, the sinter plant, the coke oven plant and the blast furnaces. Although its basic inputs are limited to coal, ores and limestones and its basic output consists of pig iron, actual operations involve a far more complex array of relationships than is suggested by this simple listing (Fig. 5.2). Among such complexities confronting the analysis are the following:

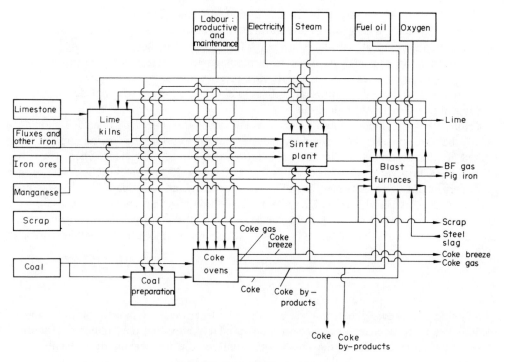

Fig. 5.2. Iron-making processes

1. Alternative flows within this department:

   For example, some coal is fed directly into coke-oven batteries while other coal is first routed through the coal-preparation plant. Similarly, some ores are conveyed directly into the blast furnaces while other ores first go through the sintering plant.

2. Internal flows within this department:

   Coke ovens feed coke and coke gas to the blast furnaces and coke breeze to the sinter plant. In addition to pig iron, blast furnaces also produce blast-furnace gas which is partly fed back into the blast furnaces and partly fed to the coke ovens and sinter plant. And limestone is used in the sinter plant as well as in the blast furnaces.

3. External flows from the department:

   While the primary product of the department is molten pig iron, blast-furnace gas and coke-oven gas are also piped into the lime kilns, steel furnaces and the reheating furnaces attached to steel rolling operations and scrap is sent on to the steel furnaces. But some departmental products also leave the works without further processing. Some coke and coke gas are transferred to a nearby chemical plant and, as will be discussed more fully later, varying quantities of coke—sometimes quite substantial—are produced for external sale.

4. Flows into the department from other parts of the Port Talbot Works:

   Among the wide array of such inputs and services may be noted limestone, electricity, gas, steam, oxygen, fuel oil and scrap.

Similar complexities were confronted in each of the other departments. As a result, it

77

would not seem unreasonable to conclude that effective application of our analytical framework to such a large-scale and intricately interwoven array of operations would demonstrate its practical usefulness over a wide range of industries. Although the data were obtained and the analyses made to encompass all of these detailed relationships and adjustments in them over time, the following presentation will concentrate solely on the major resource and product flows as well as their costs in order to avoid details unlikely to be of interest to most readers.

Before analysing input, output and cost adjustments in this department, it should be noted that adjustments in technology and equipment during the period studied were limited to the continued application of improvements already initiated earlier. Thus, two of the blast furnaces were relined and somewhat enlarged, fuel oil injection and oxygen blast enrichment were extended to additional furnaces and one blast furnace was computerized—the first in the United Kingdom. In addition, two batteries of coke ovens were rebuilt. Most important of all for the longer run was the construction of a new harbour capable of berthing ships of 100,000 d.w.t. which came into use during the spring of 1970.

Output

As indicated above, the major output of the department is molten pig iron and its secondary output is coke for sale, with other products providing only minor contributions to output. Figure 5.3 shows the combined output of the iron-making department for the 8-year period, as well as the output of its two major products. Three features are worthy of note: the declining trend over the period; the very sharp reductions during the fifth and sixth years (1968/9/70); and the disparities between the output of pig iron and of

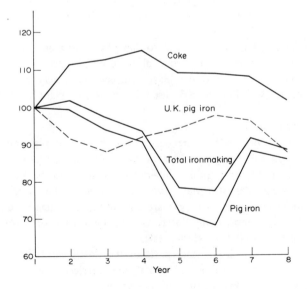

Fig. 5.3. Pig-iron production.

78

coke. In seeking explanations for these adjustments, consideration must be given to forces both outside and inside the Works.

One direct means of assessing broad external pressures would involve comparing the pig iron output of Port Talbot with that of the United Kingdom, as in Fig. 5.3. This shows that the national output fluctuated around an essentially horizontal trend, with year 7 (1970-1) closely approximating year 1 (1964-5) and the low point of year 8 (1971-2) closely approximating that of year 3 (1966-7). Thus, Port Talbot's output was in reasonably close conformity to the national pattern except during the fifth and sixth years. To explain the latter, we must look inside the plant.

The history of the plant reveals that in June 1969 the VLN (very low nitrogen) steel-making plant closed down followed by the Open Hearth plant in November 1970. Meanwhile the BOS (basic oxygen steel) plant began production in October 1969. Thus, from June until October 1969 the Open Hearth alone was manufacturing steel and it took several months before the BOS plant approached full capacity operating levels. Figure 5.4 shows the output of ingots from each of the three steel plants and total ingot output. Clearly, the modernization of steel-making caused output (and hence the consumption of pig iron) to be severely reduced during the changeover. Specifically, after closely paralleling changes in the steel output during the first 4 years studied, pig iron also declined in direct proportion to sharp declines of steel output in the fifth and sixth years. It may also be noted that pig iron production was only 15 per cent below its first-year level in the final year covered as compared with a lag of 21 per cent in the recovery of steel production. This reflected the higher ratio of pig iron inputs in basic oxygen furnaces than in open hearth furnaces, which customarily used a higher ratio of scrap to pig iron.

The remaining observation to be explained concerns the divergence between pig iron and coke production. Although coke operations are normally scheduled almost entirely to meet blast-furnace input requirements, a decline in the latter need not necessitate a

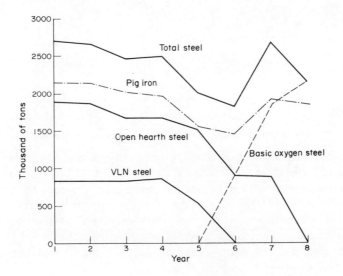

Fig. 5.4. Steel production.

79

comparable curtailment of coke-oven operations if a ready market is available for the sale of excess coke. Between years 2 and 4, average annual coke production in excess of blast furnace needs was only 68,000 tons, or about 5 per cent of total coke output. During the next 3 years, however, average annual excess coke production was raised to 266,000 or about 20 per cent of total coke output, as a policy of producing excess coke for external sale was implemented. The resulting significant impact on the output of the iron-making department is apparent in Fig. 5.3, which shows the disparity in adjustments between this total and pig iron production alone during the second half of the period studied.

To summarize, the total output of the iron-making department followed a declining trend over the 8 years in addition to undergoing an especially sharp reduction during the 2 years when older steel making processes and facilities were being replaced. And the downward trend would have been even steeper were it not for a decision to increase the production of coke for external sale.

Inputs

1. Labour. Figure 5.5 shows a decrease in total man-hours during the first half of the period followed by a sharp decline and recovery during the second half. It is interesting to note that total man-hours declined only 20 per cent at the point of minimum production as compared with a decline in total output of 24 per cent. More surprising is the finding that maintenance labour man-hours had declined at that point by one-third

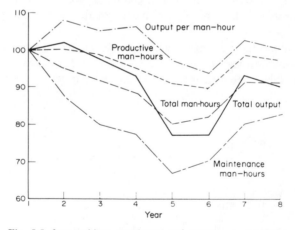

Fig. 5.5. Iron-making: man-hours and output per man-hour.

while productive man-hours had declined by only 10 per cent. Moreover, maintenance labour man-hours in the final year studied remained almost 20 per cent below that of the initial year in comparison with a decline of less than 5 per cent in productive labour man-hours. And further analysis reveals that this pattern was pervasive in all operating units of the department, except the new harbour. These findings suggest that such common shifts may have been engendered by new departmental policies. In addition, they offer a useful reminder that maintenance employment levels need not always be less flexible than those of productive labour.

As a result of such adjustments, Fig. 5.5 shows that output per man-hour for the

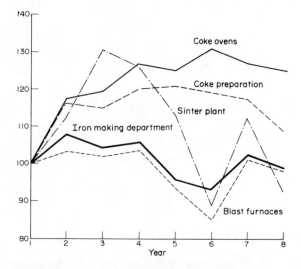

Fig. 5.6. Iron-making: output per man-hour.

department fluctuated within plus or minus 8 per cent about a horizontal trend. Further information is presented in Fig. 5.6, which shows the wide variety of adjustment patterns to be identified, diagnosed and controlled even within such a closely integrated production system. Of course, these differences are due in large measure to the divergence between coke production and pig-iron production shown in Fig. 5.3, thus accounting for the continued higher level of output per man-hour in coal preparation and coke ovens than in the sinter plant and blast furnaces. But there are other differences as well due to improvements in equipment and processes.

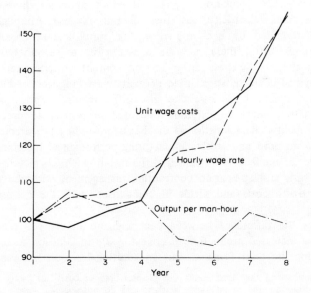

Fig. 5.7. Iron-making: output per man-hour, wage rates and unit wage costs.

81

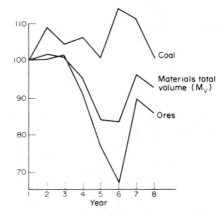

Fig. 5.8. Iron-making: materials volume and principal components.

A comparison of changes in output per man-hour with accompanying adjustments in average wages per man-hour reveals resulting changes in the department's average wage cost per unit of output. Figure 5.7 shows that wage rates rose by 8 per cent over the first 2 years, by 13 per cent over the next 3 years and by 28 per cent over the final 2 years. Because of the horizontal trend in output per man-hour, unit wage costs paralleled these sharp increases in wage rates. It is noted that labour costs[2] averaged less than 6 per cent of total costs in iron-making (Fig. 5.14) not only here but in other countries as well [3, p. 137]. Hence, even substantial changes in labour inputs may be expected to exert only a small influence on total costs.

2. Materials. Figure 5.8 shows the total volume of materials consumed by the iron-making department. This calculation covered all minor materials (limestone, fluxes and scrap) as well as fuels (electricity, gas, fuel oil and oxygen). Although the totals are overwhelmingly determined by coal and ores, this simplification disguises a far more complex situation. Actually, there may be a dozen or more varieties of iron-bearing materials entering the plant. These differ in iron content, in associated chemical constituents and in physical characteristics, often necessitating segregation or blending as well as special preparatory treatment. Because they also differ in market price and transportation costs, such alternatives must be carefully evaluated in respect to processing costs and yields as well as quality characteristics as the basis for guiding procurement efforts in the interests of improving iron and steel manufacturing performance. Incoming coal shipments may also include a number of varieties differing in such characteristics as chemical composition, strength and size—again confronting management with the need to evaluate processing productivity, costs and yields in comparison with the delivered cost of such varieties.

One reason for the difference between coal and ore inputs was identified earlier as attributable to the increased production of coke for sale in addition to serving its primary function of feeding the blast furnaces. But an additional reason is revealed by Fig. 5.9:

---

[2] It should be emphasized that throughout this chapter "labour costs" or "wages" refer only to the wages of direct production and maintenance workers and do not include wages of service personnel, employment expenses, national insurance contributions and holiday pay, or salaries.

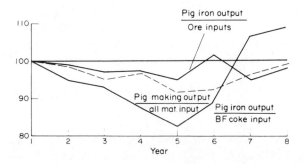

Fig. 5.9. Iron-making: materials productivity.

progressively decreasing pig iron output per ton of coke entering the blast furnaces over the first 5 years, reaching a level of 18 per cent below its origin. Only during the last 2 years did this ratio achieve new peaks. In part, this may be attributed to the record-breaking reductions in coke input requirements reached in our base year of 1964 as the result of applications of high top pressure, oil injection and oxygen blast enrichment reportedly yielding consistent increases in pig iron output per ton of coke between 20 and 30 per cent [1, p. 26]. And in part, it may be attributed to the particular mix of blast furnaces in use. Another reason is suggested by the sharp reductions in fuel oil and oxygen consumption per ton of pig iron after year 3. Thus, the decrease in pig iron output per ton of coke is traceable in considerable measure to the substitution of coke for alternative fuels. As for the sharp reversal in the trend of pig iron output per ton of coke during the last 3 years, three factors may have contributed significantly: the computerization of the largest blast furnace in 1968; the rebuilding of coke batteries with new ovens, one in 1968 and one in 1971, to yield improved coke quality; and the six-fold increase in the use of oxygen.

Variations in pig-iron output per ton of ore inputs varied more narrowly as shown in Fig. 5.9 because variations in the metal content and other characteristics of different batches of purchased ores tend to be offset by blending before smelting begins. Over the period as a whole, the total output of the iron-making department relative to inputs of all

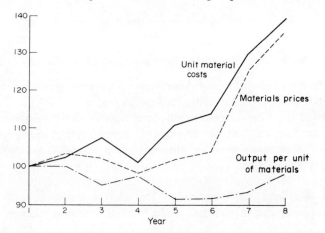

Fig. 5.10. Iron-making: materials productivity, prices and unit costs.

materials fluctuated around an essentially horizontal trend, recovering during the last 2 years most of the ground lost earlier. And in view of the sharp increases in the average prices paid for all materials combined as shown in Fig. 5.10, the absence of significant gains in the productivity of materials ensured that unit material costs would rise in step with such prices. Unlike the increases in unit wage costs, however, increases in unit material costs represented a heavy burden because they average almost 70 per cent of all costs in this department as shown in Fig. 5.14.

3. Capital. The fixed investments within the scope of the iron-making department consist primarily of the harbour installations, coal-preparation and sinter plants, coke-oven batteries, blast furnaces and the transportation facilities connecting these. Although the Works as a whole was relatively old, successive development programmes had periodically upgraded most major facilities. Moreover, as was mentioned in the introductory remarks about the iron-making department, an investment of about £20 million was made during the period under study in developing a deep-water harbour and another £5 million in improving ore preparation, coke-oven and blast furnace facilities. While the harbour project was designed to facilitate access to overseas ore and coal at the lower delivered prices made possible by large ships, rather than to increase productive capacity, the latter was enhanced modestly by the facilities improvements just mentioned. Net fixed investment tended to keep declining, of course, as a result of depreciation charges except for the new infusions necessitated by the improvement programme, as shown in Fig. 5.11. As a

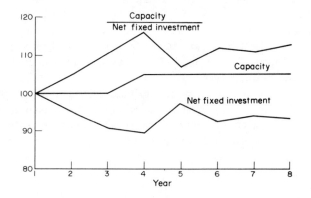

Fig. 5.11. Iron-making: capacity, net fixed investment and productivity of capital.

result, the productivity of net fixed investment fluctuated around a horizontal trend during years 3 to 8 at 10 per cent above its level in year 1.

Because much of the heavy facilities and equipment in the iron-making department is old enough to have been substantially depreciated, depreciation charges[3] averaged less than 5 per cent of total costs, contrary to widespread impressions about their magnitudes in such capital intensive operations.

4. Total unit costs and cost proportions. The relative change in total unit costs over any period may be regarded as the product of the relative change in each of its

[3] Measured at historical costs.

component categories multiplied by its share of total costs at the beginning of the period.

$$\left(\Delta\frac{\text{Total costs}}{\text{Output}}\right)_{2,1} = \left[\left(\Delta\frac{\text{Material costs}}{\text{Output}}\right)_{2,1} \times \left(\frac{\text{Material cost}}{\text{Total cost}}\right)_{1}\right] + \left[\left(\Delta\frac{\text{Wages}}{\text{Output}}\right)_{2,1} \times\right.$$

$$\left.\times \left(\frac{\text{Wages}}{\text{Total cost}}\right)_{1}\right] + \left[\left(\Delta\frac{\text{Other costs}}{\text{Output}}\right)_{2,1} \times \left(\frac{\text{Other costs}}{\text{Total cost}}\right)_{1}\right].$$

Figure 5.12 presents the relative changes in the major cost components and Fig. 5.14 represents their relative magnitudes.

Although the increase in unit material costs led the increase in unit wage costs between years 1 and 3, they moved very closely together thereafter. Other expenses, which include salaries and overheads rose far more rapidly per unit of output during the first half of the period when the harbour and other capital improvement projects were under way, but

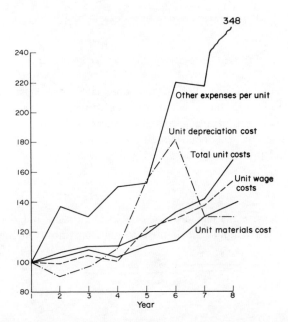

Fig. 5.12. Iron-making: total unit costs and major components.

rejoined the pattern of the other unit costs towards the end. It should be emphasized, however, that total unit costs were overwhelmingly dominated by material costs and that the pattern of cost proportions remained remarkably stable despite major adjustments in output and in factor prices as well as the introduction of technical modifications in various facilities.

Conclusions

Productivity changes in the iron-making department were relatively modest during the period except for the decreases in the productivity of labour and of materials engendered by the reduction in steel output during the changeover to the basic oxygen process. The productivity of capital, as measured by the ratio of capacity to net fixed investment, rose because continuing depreciation more than offset new investments. But the potential cost benefits of this gain were more than offset by the sharp decrease in the rate of capacity utilization, which was more than 25 per cent lower in years 5 and 6 than in year 1 and was still 14 per cent below the latter in the final year. As for input factor proportions, the most significant changes were reductions in the ratio of actively utilized capital (net fixed investment multiplied by the ratio of output to capacity) both to labour and materials because of the rigidity of capacity relative to the flexibility of labour and materials inputs under conditions of reduced output (Fig. 5.13).

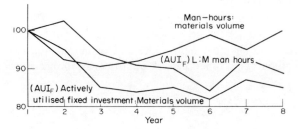

Fig. 5.13. Iron-making: input factor proportions.

Market developments outside the Works dominated unit cost adjustments in this department not only through the effect of reduced demand on the productivity of inputs but also through the effect of rising materials prices and wage rates. As a result, the period ended before general economic conditions permitted realization of the full benefits of the innovations and investments made during these years.

II. Steel-making

The steel-making department includes not only steel furnaces but the universal slab mill as well. Its major material inputs are limited to pig iron (mostly molten), steel scrap and

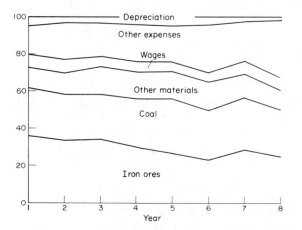

Fig. 5.14. Iron-making: cost proportions.

oxygen as well as other fuels. These are cooked in furnaces to produce molten steel which is poured into ingot moulds to cool. With minor exceptions, these ingots are then rolled into slabs in the universal mill before being transferred to the finishing department. Accordingly, this department is characterized by a simpler array of processes and flows than the other two. On the other hand, it was subjected to far greater technological innovations than the others—thus offering another kind of test of the applicability of the productivity network analysis model which has been proposed.

Three steel-making processes were in use during the period studied: the long-established Open-hearth process; a modified Bessemer (very low nitrogen—VLN) process which had been introduced in 1959 to process high phosphorus ores; and the new Basic Oxygen Steel (BOS) process which began working in October 1969. The VLN plant was closed in July 1969 because the expected benefits of processing high phosphorus ores were never fully realized. And the open-hearth furnaces were closed in November 1970 after the BOS plant demonstrated its readiness to assume the full load. The basic reason for this change over was the expectation, based on the experience of modern American, Japanese and European plants, that the BOS process' ten-fold increase in the speed of steel-making would substantially reduce operating costs, manning levels and capital requirements per ton of capacity.

Output

Almost the entire output of this department takes the form of mild steel and silicon steel slabs to be transferred to the finishing department. The actual adjustments confirm the general pattern foreshadowed by earlier discussion of the changing composition and aggregate level of steel furnace output (Fig. 5.4) except for the less pronounced recovery of total departmental output after the changeover to the BOS process. This is shown in Fig. 5.15 along with the differences between adjustments in the two series which are attributable to the building up or drawing down of steel ingot inventories and to variations in the direct sale of ingots. Incidentally, the consistently higher level of steel department output indexes than those for steel furnace output, except in years 1 and 7, seems attributable to an unusual deviation between them in the base year.

Inputs

1. Labour. During years 1 to 6, total man-hours followed the same general downward pattern as the department's total steel output, as shown in Fig. 5.15, though declining somewhat more rapidly. Thereafter, however, although output recovered about half of its loss, total man-hours continued to decline sharply, thus yielding comparably large increases in output per man-hour.

In probing for the locus of these manpower savings, one clue is provided by Fig. 5.15 which shows that maintenance man-hours declined about four times as much as productive man-hours between years 1 and 6. More detailed scrutiny of the data reveals that such sharper curtailment of maintenance labour inputs characterized all parts of the department, thus reflecting the same managerial pressure as was found in the iron-making department.

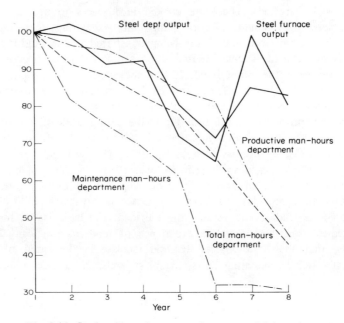

Fig. 5.15. Steel-making: departmental output and labour inputs.

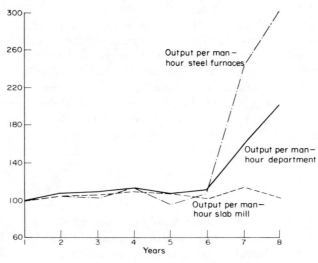

Fig. 5.16. Steel-making: output per man-hour.

Much more valuable insights, however, are provided by Fig. 5.16. This shows not only that significant increases in departmental output per man-hour occurred only during the last 2 years, but also that virtually all of the gain came from the steel furnace sector of the department. There was no significant gain in output per man-hour during years 1 to 5, however, when only open-hearth and VLN furnaces were operating. And output per man-hour in open-hearth furnaces actually declined during their remaining 2 years. Hence, all of the gain in output per man-hour was generated by the BOS plant alone, whose output per man-hour in the last year studied was three times as great as the best annual performance of the open-hearth furnaces during the 8-year period. And even further gains could be expected—for the BOS plant had a planned capacity of 3.25 million tons per year in comparison with the year 8 output of less than 2.2 million tons. Thus, managerial hopes in respect to manpower economies seemed well on the way towards full realization.

Were such gains sufficient to offset the substantial increases in wage rates which were pervasive in the industry and even more broadly? Figure 5.17 shows that wage rates rose

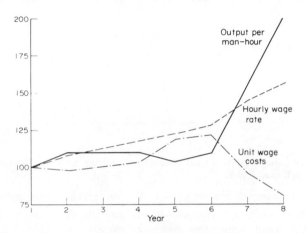

Fig. 5.17. Steel-making: output per man-hour, hourly wage rates and unit wage costs.

by about 27 per cent over the first 6 years and by another 22 per cent in the last 2 years. Increases in output per man-hour kept unit wage costs in check until year 4, but such productivity failed to keep pace with the continuing rise in wage rates over the remaining 2 years before the changeover to BOS steel-making. Thereafter, the enormous increase in output per man-hour served not only to offset increasing wage rates, but to reduce unit wage costs by one-third—unlike the experience of the iron-making department.

Lest the benefits of such gains be over-estimated, however, it should be noted that direct labour costs (as defined earlier, see footnote 2) accounted for less than 4 per cent of the total costs in this department even at the beginning of the period. On the other hand, even reductions of 1 per cent in total costs assume significant proportions when profit margins are of the order of 5 per cent or less, as has occurred in these Works in recent years (see Chapter 6).

2. *Materials.* The productivity of material inputs is affected both by the effectiveness with which individual materials are used and by substitutions of materials for one another. The basic inputs into this department may be divided into ferrous materials and fuels and the former consists primarily of pig iron and scrap while the major fuels include fuel oil, blast furnace and coke gas and high purity oxygen. As a result of the changeover in processes, changes in the composition both of ferrous and of fuel inputs far overshadowed any changes in the effectiveness with which individual inputs were used.

Figure 5.18 shows that the index of combined materials input volume moved in very

89

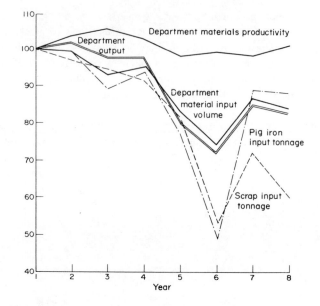

Fig. 5.18. Steel-making department: output, volume of materials input and productivity of materials, tonnage of pig-iron and scrap inputs.

close accord with changes in the output of the steel-making department throughout the period studied. As a result, the productivity of materials inputs fluctuated very narrowly around a horizontal trend, responding only very slightly even to the sharp reductions in output during years 5 and 6. Further examination reveals both that the two major ferrous inputs moved in unison except for the last 2 years and also that they declined far more sharply in year 6 than departmental input. The latter is attributable partly to the fact that steel furnace output—which is the immediate product of pig iron and scrap inputs— declined substantially more than the final output of the department in the form largely of slabs (see Fig. 5.15).

But the sharper decline in scrap than in pig-iron inputs was clearly due to the shift in processes. As shown in Fig. 5.19, the scrap rate averaged about 40 per cent in open

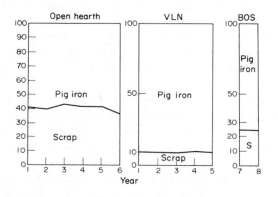

Fig. 5.19. Ratio of scrap to pig-iron inputs by steel process.

90

hearths, just under 10 per cent in the VLN process and about 25 per cent in the BOS plant. Hence, so long as the open hearth accounted for 70 per cent or more of total output, leaving less than 30 per cent for the VLN, the overall scrap ratio hovered about 31 per cent as compared with 26 and 24 per cent, respectively, in the last 2 years when the BOS plant took over.

Even greater shifts developed in the composition of fuel inputs, again primarily because of the changeover in processes. Fuel oil accounted for more than two-thirds of fuel costs in the open hearth but was eliminated in the BOS plant. On the other hand, high-purity oxygen accounted for less than one-third of fuel costs in the open hearth but rose to well over 90 per cent in the BOS plant (Fig. 5.20).

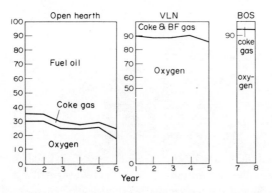

Fig. 5.20. Composition of fuel input costs by steel process.

The average price of all material inputs rose by only 5 per cent during years 1 to 5 as shown in Fig. 5.21 and unit materials cost lagged these increases until the fifth year because of the slight increase in the level of materials productivity. Thereafter, materials productivity fell to slightly below its original level and materials prices rose more rapidly to drive unit material cost upward on a parallel course. It should be recognized that the observed increases in the average price of all materials are attributable not only to increases in the price of each input, but also to the fact mentioned earlier that the conversion to the BOS process involved the replacement of lower-priced fuel oil by higher-priced oxygen and of lower-priced scrap by a higher ratio of more costly pig iron.

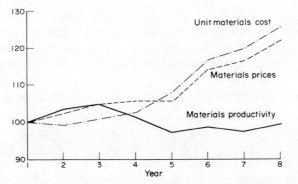

Fig. 5.21. Steel-making: materials unit cost, prices and productivity.

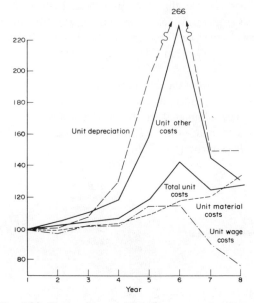

Fig. 5.22. Steel-making: total and component unit costs.

Similarly, the apparent reduction in the productivity of materials inputs is largely attributable to an increase in the proportion of total inputs weighted by relatively higher prices rather than to any reduction in the technical efficiency of given conversion processes.

In short, changes in total material costs per unit of steel output are the resultant of changes in pig iron, scrap and other unit costs weighted by their respective shares of total material costs.[4] During the first 3 years, unit material costs rose slightly because substantial increases of about one-third in "other materials" were diluted in their effects because of the small proportion of material costs attributable to them. During the next 3 years, doubling of "other material costs" contributed equally with small increases in pig-iron costs (which are weighted by a much larger proportion of total material costs) to raise unit material costs. And during the last 2 years, a sharp increase in pig-iron costs far overshadowed substantial decreases in scrap costs and other costs to raise unit material costs again.

3. Capital and other costs. The replacement of open-hearth and VLN facilities by the BOS plant involved investments of the order of £18.5 million with attendant sharp increases in depreciation charges. In addition, the changeover was accompanied by heavy though fortunately short-lived increases in "other costs" and in depreciation charges. These loomed especially large in terms of unit costs both because the innovation was not designed to increase capacity despite the heavy commitments made and because depart-

[4] The decomposition of materials costs may be done as follows:

$$\left(\Delta\,\frac{M}{PO}\right)_{2,1} = \left[\left(\Delta\,\frac{M_S}{PO}\right)_{2,1}\left(\frac{M_S}{M}\right)_1\right] + \left[\left(\Delta\,\frac{M_{pi}}{PO}\right)_{2,1}\left(\frac{M_{pi}}{M}\right)_1\right] + \left[\left(\Delta\frac{M_O}{PO}\right)_{2,1}\left(\frac{M_O}{M}\right)_1\right]$$

where M = total material costs; M_S = scrap costs; M_{pi} = pig iron costs; M_O = other materials; PO = physical output and subscripts 1 and 2 represent the beginning and end of the period.

mental output dropped sharply during the changeover and failed to regain even its initial levels by the end of the period studied.

Resulting changes in these unit costs are shown in Fig. 5.22. One must hasten to call attention to Fig. 5.23, however, to put these burdens in a proper perspective by comparing their magnitudes with other outlays. Thus, despite their sharp increases per unit of output, depreciation charges accounted for less than 4 per cent of total costs even at their peak. On the other hand, "other costs" far overshadow wage costs in magnitude and yet seem to be accorded much less aggressive attention.

Total Unit Costs

Figure 5.24 shows that total unit costs in steel-making rose less than 6 per cent between years 1 and 4, but rose by one-third during the next 2 years before declining by 10 per cent over the last 2 years. This outcome was traceable to quite disparate adjustment patterns among its major components, especially during the last 4 years. During years 5 and 6, increases in unit material and unit wage costs were far surpassed by increases in other costs and depreciation charges per unit. During years 7 and 8, increases in unit material costs were sufficient to more than offset sharp reductions in other cost categories. As a result, total unit costs at the end of the period were about one-quarter above their level 7 years earlier. But most of this increase was clearly attributable to inflationary pressures transmitted through input factor prices, as has been noted. It is also noteworthy that cost proportions were almost the same in year 8 as in year 1 (see Fig. 5.23).

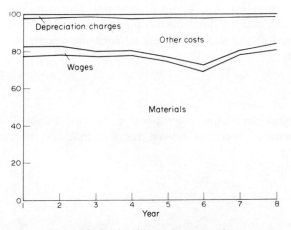

Fig. 5.23. Steel-making: cost proportions.

Conclusion

In seeking to evaluate the changeover to the BOS process, one may begin by noting that the British Iron and Steel Federation estimated [2, p. 38] that, under certain assumptions concerning capacity and scrap usage, conversion costs per ton should be 20 per cent lower when using the basic oxygen process than for an open hearth. Obviously, nothing of this sort was achieved during the period under study, even if one were to exclude the effects of increases in input factor prices. The decrease in the productivity of materials, attributable primarily to the need for a higher ratio of more costly pig iron, virtually offset the cost benefits of the sharp increase in the productivity of labour, leaving additional increases in capital charges and in "other costs" as further burdens.

What accounts for such results? One important factor is that the study ended only 2½ years after the BOS plant began operating. This suggests that further improvements in performance could be expected as a result of the stream of facilitating adjustments in materials handling, furnace operation, down-time and waste control which tends to follow in the wake of major technical innovations. A possibly more important factor is the 22 per cent reduction in steel output in period 8 as compared to period 1. Overhead allocations and capital charges per unit tend to vary inversely with variations in the level of output. Hence, fuller utilization of the productive capacity may be expected to yield significant reductions in unit costs relative to what they would have been using the older processes with current factor prices—and the magnitude of such potentials is indicated by the fact that the BOS plant was capable of producing one-third more than its output in year 8. Moreover, the replacement of largely depreciated facilities with even more efficient but undepreciated facilities tends to increase unit capital charges at comparable levels of output in the short run, but may be expected to yield reduced average capital costs per unit of output as the net investment continues to be reduced through depreciation charges.

In short, the analytical model which has been used lends itself readily to the evaluation not only of productivity adjustments but also of the technological innovations which engender changes in input–output relationships and costs. And it has proved feasible to make such analyses not only at the level of component departments within a plant but even at the level of operating units within departments, thus permitting a sharper focus in identifying the specific loci of productivity adjustments and a more detailed tracing of their interacting physical and financial effects on adjoining operations as well as on higher levels of aggregation.

III. Finishing

The remaining major production component of the Port Talbot Works is the Finishing Department. It covers all processes beyond the slab mill: the hot and cold mills, the

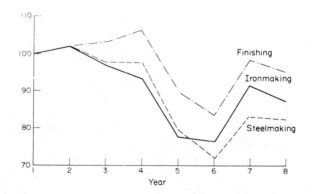

Fig. 5.24. Output of the iron-making, steel-making and finishing departments.

"heavy gauge" or "hot sheet finishing" section and the two coated products lines: Dragonite and Dragonzin. From the standpoint of productivity analysis, this department presents problems which differ from those of iron-making and steel-making by combining simple inputs (overwhelmingly slabs) with a complex array of outputs including: hot rolled plate, sheet and coil (pickled and unpickled); cold rolled coil; and coated coil and sheet (flat and corrugated). Moreover, each of these products is produced in a variety of widths and gauges to suit customer requirements. Even after consolidating this array in the interests of simplifying the analysis, account was taken of eighteen product groups.

The only significant technological change in this department was the conversion of the cold mill from 4 stands to 5 and the associated computerization of cold mill operations between 1967 and 1968 (year 4). These innovations were not far-reaching enough to warrant separate analysis of each in this report, although they did involve investments approximating £5 million.

Output

As has been the case throughout this study, changes in total output were determined by weighting changes in the output of each product category by its average price. The result, as shown in Fig. 5.24, reveals successive small increases in Finishing output between years 1 and 4 totalling 6 per cent, while steel-making output had declined by nearly 4 per cent. During the changeover in steel processes over the next 2 years, Finishing declined to 15 per cent below year 1 while steel-making dropped almost twice as much. And this gap remained during the last 2 years as Finishing averaged above 96 per cent of its initial level while steel-making averaged about 84 per cent of its initial level. Such differences in output patterns within an integrated plant are attributable to two primary factors. First provisions are obviously made to adjust for expected differential adjustments in successive operations through building up and drawing down intermediate inventories (e.g. of steel ingots and of slabs). Second, outputs are also responsive to any shifts in the composition of final products whose prices reflect differing amounts of processing.

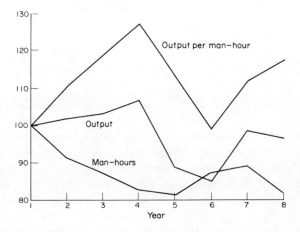

Fig. 5.25. Finishing: output, man-hours and output per man-hour.

Inputs

1. Labour. In rolling-mill operations, labour's functions tend to centre around starting, stopping, adjusting and maintaining the equipment and, hence, manning tends to be fairly stable, short of extreme fluctuations of output, except for occasional reorganizations of tasks and operations. The Finishing department also includes certain ancillary activities, especially movements into and out of inventories as well as preparations for shipment which tend to be more responsive to changes in output.

As shown in Fig. 5.25, total labour inputs declined by nearly 15 per cent between years 1 and 3 and thereafter fluctuated around the expected essentially horizontal trend. The initial decline was obviously attributable to the steady pressure to reduce man-hour requirements which was reflected by all three departments during the first 4 years. Lesser fluctuations thereafter may have been attributable to such localized developments as: the need to adjust productive and maintenance labour inputs to handle the additional stand of rolls in the cold mill as well as the associated computerized controls; and the need to handle the increased volume of inventory adjustments necessitated by deviations between output levels in steel and in finishing. Nevertheless, maintenance labour was reduced more sharply than productive labour in this department as well.

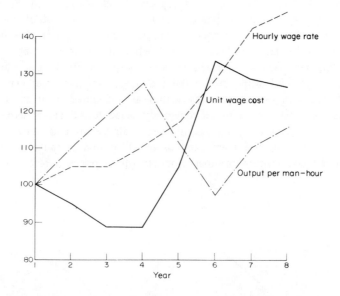

Fig. 5.26. Finishing: output per man-hour, hourly wage rate and unit wage cost.

After the sharp increase in labour productivity between years 1 and 4, it declined and rose again—roughly paralleling variations in output, except for the last year. Because output per man-hour had risen by more than one-fourth while hourly wage rates had risen by only one-eighth by year 4, unit wage costs declined by about one-eighth over that period (Fig. 5.26). During the next 2 years, unit wage costs rose by half as a sharp drop in output per man-hour, attributable to a comparable decrease in output, was augmented by a substantial increase in wage rates. During the last 2 years, unit wage costs actually

96

declined modestly because a 20 per cent increase in labour productivity more than offset accompanying increases in wage rates.

Lest the significance of such adjustments should be over-emphasized, however, it should be noted that wage costs averaged only about 4 per cent of total costs in this department (but note that these wages are limited to direct labour only, as defined in footnote 2).

2. Materials. As was noted earlier, material inputs into this department are dominated by slabs and the ratio of output to inputs can be altered only to the modest extent possible by reducing waste in heating, defective products and scrap, and by altering the product-mix. Actually, the volume of materials input varied almost exactly with output, keeping the productivity of materials within 1 per cent of its level in year 1 throughout the period. Hence, increases in the average price of materials (i.e. primarily the cost or transfer price of slabs) were transmitted to unit material costs, which were 6-7 per cent above the base year during years 3 to 5 and then rose by another 17 per cent over the next 2 years before dropping slightly at the end. The importance of this pattern is apparent from the fact that materials accounted for 82 per cent of total costs in this department.

3. Depreciation and other costs. Net fixed investment tended to decline steadily, of course, because of depreciation charges, except for the additional investments, mostly in year 4, to expand and computerize the cold mill and to make some improvements in galvanizing operations. Accordingly, the productivity of net fixed investment tended to rise steadily, except for the period of new investment, as shown in Fig. 5.27. But the introduction of new undepreciated investments increased the rate of depreciation and this combined with decreased output to raise depreciation charges per unit of output. Once again, however, the effects of such adjustments are brought into more meaningful perspectives by noting that depreciation averaged less than 2 per cent of total costs in this department.

"Other expenses", which it may be recalled include salaries and overheads, rose more than any other major category of costs during the period as a whole, averaging about

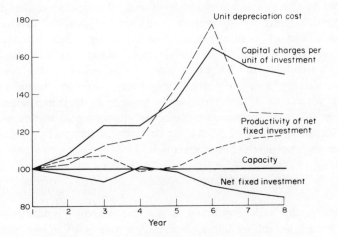

Fig. 5.27. Finishing: capacity, net fixed investment, productivity of net fixed investment.

two-thirds above its initial level during the last 3 years. Moreover, it accounted for twice as large a proportion of total costs as wages and depreciation charges combined, averaging about 12 per cent.

Total Unit Costs

Figure 5.28 reveals considerable differences among the component categories of unit cost. The dominance of materials is apparent from the fact that it alone closely paralleled total unit costs throughout. Yet the possibilities of substantially lowering material costs through managerial efforts in this department are very narrowly limited by the fact that the greatest part of such costs represent the transfer prices of slabs received from the steel-making department.

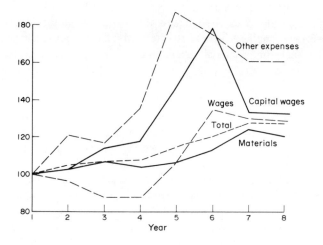

Fig. 5.28. Finishing: total unit costs and major components.

Changes in unit costs are attributable, of course, to changes in input factor prices and in the quantities of these factors employed per unit of output—and changes in the latter are usually traceable either to adjustments in output levels, in the case of inputs which are relatively inflexible, or to adjustments in the technology, organization and manning of major production tasks. Among these three factors, changes in unit material costs were almost entirely attributable to changes in input factor prices. In the case of unit wage costs, all three factors were influential: wage rate increases throughout; changes in manning during years 1 to 4; and variations in input levels thereafter. And in the case of depreciation, too, all three factors were important: increasing depreciation charges during years 1 to 6; increasing inputs of capital due to technical improvements during years 3 to 5; and variations in input levels during years 4 to 7.

Conclusion

Methodologically, the basic conclusion is that the proposed productivity network and cost structure model proved readily applicable to a variety of highly complex industrial operations both in terms of the concepts involved and in terms of the availability of the data required as a by-product of existing managerial planning and control functions. Hence, it seems eminently practicable to apply the model to a wide range of industries at relatively small cost in the interests of providing additional valuable guides for managerial evaluations of past performance or of prospective alternatives. It should also be noted in this connection that the model readily lends itself to further elaboration either in the interests of probing progressively small sectors of operation or in the interests of exploring more fully the alternative means of effecting given functional purposes. The former has been illustrated through examining separate units within the iron-making and steel-making departments. And approaches to analysing functional alternatives were suggested in connection with the analysis of different combinations of fuels and of ferrous inputs into blast furnaces.

Analytically, one basic conclusion centres around the importance of recognizing the wide diversity of patterns even within a tightly integrated plant: as among departments; as among components within each department; and as among the relative prices and productivities of different inputs. A second basic conclusion involves the importance of recognizing the widely different ranges within which successive departments in a sequence of production operations can alter performance and costs within the constraints imposed on them. A third conclusion suggests the importance for strategic planning of considering not only the possible reductions which might be achieved in respect to various input factors or different departments, but also the relative importance of such factors and the extent to which improvements in departments come early in the chain of operations, and thus yield widely diffused benefits, or come in the final stages. And finally the analysis suggests something of the length of time which may be necessary to effect the expected benefits of major innovations.

References

1. Brinn, D. (1972) *Development of Iron and Steel Industry in the Port Talbot Area.* British Steel Corporation, Port Talbot, June.
2. British Iron & Steel Federation, Development Coordinating Committee (July 1966) *Stage 1 report.*
3. Gold, B. (1971) *Explorations in Managerial Economics: Productivity, Costs, Technology and Growth.* Macmillan, London; Basic Books, New York.

CHAPTER 6

An Integrated Steel Plant

SAMUEL EILON, BELA GOLD and JUDITH SOESAN

The case studies in Chapter 5 illustrate productivity analyses at the departmental level within a plant. The Port Talbot plant is described by the simplified diagram 5.1, and the schematic division of the plant into three production departments plus services (which may be regarded as a separate department for our purposes) is given in Fig. 6.1.

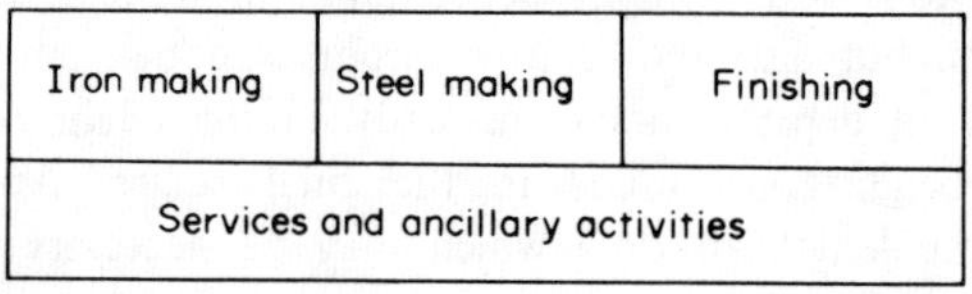

Iron making	Steel making	Finishing
Services and ancillary activities		

Fig. 6.1. A schematic division of the plant.

The purpose of this chapter is to show how the productivity analysis model can be applied to the plant as a whole, which may be considered here as a single entity with numerous inputs and outputs (see Fig. 6.2), although we shall concentrate our attention only on the major outputs of the plant, while subsidiary activities (such as electricity generation, coke oven by-product purification, etc.) will not be analysed. Also, at the plant level we can extend our considerations to include the managerial control ratios discussed in Chapter 2 (see Fig. 2.5). This could not be done at the level of the individual departments since the concept of profit was not a meaningful one at any level

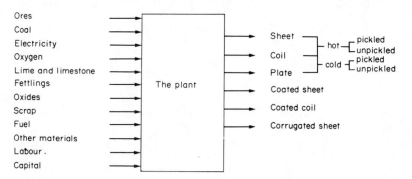

Fig. 6.2. The plant–inputs and major outputs (in addition, there are outputs of coke, steel ingots and slabs).

100

lower than that of the whole works. Even for the latter it must be stressed that the plant is part of BSC and hence not free to fix its own pricing schedules and that the value of its turnover and its profit margins are therefore not totally within its own control. Nevertheless, managerial control ratios of the type illustrated in Fig. 2.5 will be of use to senior management in assessing the performance of the plant and in evaluating the wisdom or otherwise of past investment decisions.

First, we examine in this case study the productivity relationships and the cost structure, on the lines of the analyses in the previous two chapters. The managerial control ratios are then described and discussed, and in the last section of this chapter various questions are examined concerning the performance of the plant and the possible effect of certain events and decisions on this performance.

Productivity Ratios

One commonly used measure of the capacity of the plant as a whole is its capacity to produce ingot steel,[1] as this represents a central stage in the series of sequential processes in the plant. Over the 8-year period under study, this capacity fell by 10 per cent (see Fig. 6.3) with the closure of the VLN and then the open-hearth processes, and output fell

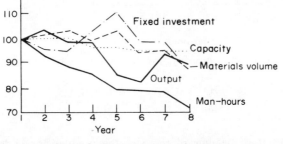

Fig. 6.3. Physical input and outputs.

by 10.6 per cent with the lowest level (17.7 per cent below the first year) occurring in the sixth year. Man-hours too followed a steady downward trend, falling 27.8 per cent over the whole period, and the volume of materials used also fell, but only by 14 per cent. The value of net fixed investment recorded a dramatic increase from year 3 to year 5, when major expenditure on a BOS plant and a new harbour took place, and then declined to 87.6 per cent of its original level.

In considering these data it may be useful to start with an analysis of the factors associated with changes in physical output per man-hour, since this ratio is quoted so often and so misleadingly, both by the press and by more learned sources. The network of productivity relationships used in the model reminds us that changes in the productivity of any input (in this case labour) may be attributable to changes in its use proportional to another input (materials or capital) and to changes in the productivity of that input. Thus, labour productivity may increase because new labour-saving equipment or facilities have been introduced. This would be reflected in the ratio of labour to

---

[1] At different periods this would be equivalent to the capacity, or capacities, of the open hearth plus the VLN, the open hearth alone, or the BOS plant (see Fig. 5.4).

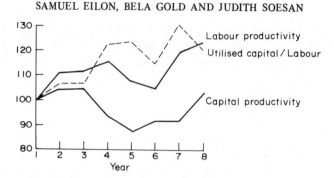

Fig. 6.4. The relationship between labour and capital.

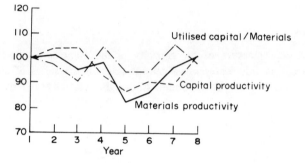

Fig. 6.5. The relationship between materials and capital.

actively utilized capital and possibly in the productivity of capital (CAP/I_F), hence

$$\frac{PO}{M\text{-}hr} \equiv \frac{CAP}{I_F} \times \frac{I_F \times PO/CAP}{M\text{-}hr}$$

Thus, Fig. 6.4 shows that the upward trend in the productivity of labour is due to the increase in actively utilized fixed investment in relation to labour.[2] However, sharp decreases in the productivity of capital in years 3 and 4 helped to hold down increases in labour productivity and even to decrease it.

Turning to the productivity of materials, it would be useful to assess the effects, if any, of the opening of the new harbour and of the replacement of older steel processes by the BOS plant, which took place during 1969/70, by

$$\frac{PO}{M_V} = \frac{CAP}{I_F} \times \frac{I_F \times PO/CAP}{M_V}$$

Figure 6.5 shows a horizontal trend in the productivity of materials (PO/M_v) until year 4 followed by a sharp reduction in year 5 and by an upward trend thereafter. This resulted from offsetting adjustments in the productivity of capital (CAP/I_F) and in actively utilized fixed investment. In year 5 both factors drove the productivity of materials downward. Thereafter, increases in capital productivity and in the ratio of utilized capital to materials alternated in raising the productivity of materials beyond its initial level.

[2] The coefficient of correlation between the two is 0.64.

102

If we then look in more detail at the productivity of capital, we see in Figs. 6.3 and 6.4 that its variations were largely attributable to changes in fixed investment, with some change in capacity. The very low productivity of capital in year 5 was caused by the large amount of investment to *replace* existing capital rather than to provide additional capacity. The fluctuations in the utilization rate (PO/CAP) followed changes in output, and actively utilized fixed investment, therefore, did not rise, resulting in the ratio of actively utilized fixed investment to materials remaining fairly static.

The Structure of Costs

It may be helpful in our analysis of the structure of costs at Port Talbot to bear in mind six pervading assumptions [1, pp. 95-96] that appear to have gained widespread acceptance:

(1) "that manufacturing wage costs account for the greater part of the selling price of products in most manufacturing industries;

(2) that the increasing efficiency of production processes and the more thorough utilization of by-products have led to a progressive and substantial reduction in the ratio of cost of materials to the selling price of manufactured goods;

(3) that sharply increased production per man-hour, attributable largely to more extensive mechanization and more effective management controls, has steadily reduced the relative importance of wage costs in total product costs;

(4) that the proportion of total selling price accounted for by salaries, overheads and profits has risen significantly as a result of the combined effects of a higher ratio of managerial and technical personnel to wage earners, of the increased overhead costs attendant on heavier mechanization, and of the maintenance or

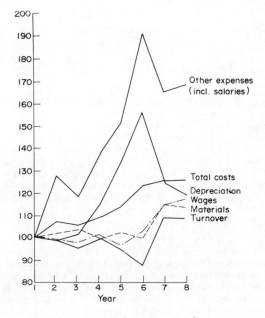

Fig. 6.6. Total and factor costs and turnover.

103

expansion of profits presumed to have supplied the necessary incentive to further investment in technological improvements;" also

(5) "that, because of frequent fluctuations in raw material prices, wage rates, profit margins and levels of production, the internal composition of manufacturing costs is subject to continuous and substantial variation;" and

(6) that total unit cost is inversely related to output level.

Because these expectations were found not to be true of the iron and steel industry in the U.S. over an extended, though earlier period, it seems useful to learn whether or not these assumptions are supported by the Port Talbot data by looking at the performance of total costs, cost proportions and unit costs in turn.

Changes in Turnover, Total Costs and Cost Proportions

The total turnover over the period rose by 8.2 per cent but the increase was by no means steady, as Fig. 6.6 shows. Total costs rose much more steadily after a slight fall in year 3, while the fluctuations in the cost components of total cost were as marked as those in turnover and were not always in the same direction. It is, therefore, not surprising that the cost proportions and turnover proportions were not stable (see Figs. 6.7a and 6.7b), especially in the unusual year 6, when output slumped because of the changeover to the BOS plant.[3]

A second interesting point concerning cost proportions is their relative magnitudes. The share of wages averages 17.5 per cent of total costs,[4] and wages plus salaries averaged 23.9 per cent, but at least twice as much was spent on materials, which averaged 49.2 per cent of total costs. For the purpose of a detailed analysis, the share of "other expenses" is, alas, high and it would have been desirable to split this category into several components. Depreciation turns out to be surprisingly low (averaging 6.1 per cent of total costs), so that there is no evidence of the dominance of depreciation in total costs, a widespread belief concerning the iron and steel industry in general.

Changes in Unit Price and Unit Costs

(a) Trends. If we examine the relationship between turnover (value of product) and the

[3] The change in the accounting system in 1969/70 (year 6) led to a "6-month year" (from October 1969 to March 1970). In order to produce comparable data for this year, the figures available for the 6 months were doubled to extend the "6-month year" to a normal 12-month year. This weighting procedure makes the implicit assumption that the conditions prevailing during the 6-month interval were representative of the whole year. However, year 6 marked the changeover to the BOS plant, and this change—coupled with prolonged industrial unrest—resulted in exceptionally low performance, with output and turnover at their lowest levels, thereby tending to exaggerate the results for year 6 as a whole.

[4] It should be noted that labour costs in this chapter are not comparable with those shown in the previous chapter. In the departmental analysis in Chapter 5 only direct wages for production and maintenance workers were accounted for, and these excluded all other employment costs, holidays and national insurance (all of which were included in "other expenses"). However, for the plant as a whole "wages" account for all direct production and maintenance workers, as well as various workers providing services and generating electricity and steam which are not included in the materials input (all these amounted to an average of 14.3 per cent of total turnover) plus employment costs (recorded as 2.6 per cent of turnover on average); thus total wages come to 16.9 per cent of turnover, while average salaries for the 8-year period amounted to an additional 6.1 per cent.

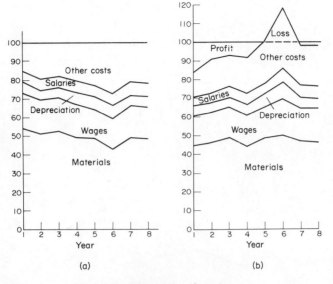

Fig. 6.7a. Proportions of total costs.
Fig. 6.7b. Proportions of turnover.

volume of physical output, we can analyse fluctuations in average selling price per unit of output and the contributions of changes in both output and average selling price to changes in turnover. Figure 6.8 shows that the average selling price rose almost steadily after year 2 and was 21.1 per cent higher at the end of the period than at the beginning. Over the same period, turnover increased by some 8.2 per cent but output fell by 10.6 per cent. (Turnover was at its lowest in year 6, when both output and average selling price fell relative to the previous year.) Thus, the increase in turnover during the period was due to price inflation; that it did not rise more was because of the fall in output.

Figure 6.9 shows that unit costs of wages, material, depreciation and other expenses (including salaries) rose by 30.8, 26.4, 33.7 and 88.5 per cent, respectively. Depreciation and other unit costs peaked in year 6 when the major initial capital and running-in costs of the BOS plant were incurred and when output fell sharply,[5] so that these fixed costs could not be spread. Unit wage costs also rose significantly in this year while unit material costs were as in year 5, suggesting that the total wage bill is relatively fixed in nature (wages in Fig. 6.6 were relatively stationary during the first 5 years, rising to

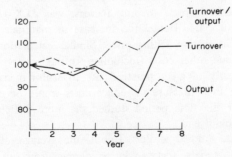

Fig. 6.8. The calculation of average selling price.

[5] For the other special features of year 6 see footnote 3.

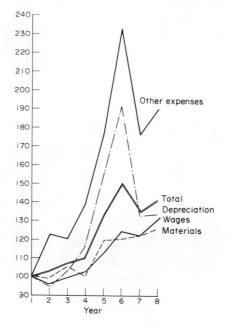

Fig. 6.9. Unit costs.

another plateau in the last 2 years). Total unit costs rose by 40.9 per cent over the period, the major increase occurring in the last 4 years (see Fig. 6.9).

(b) Relative effects of cost adjustments on price. In theory it is possible to estimate the relative contribution of each cost factor to any change in average selling price; if the change in unit cost is weighted by its proportionate share in turnover at the beginning of the period and all such weighted changes are summed, it will give the change in average selling price. The weighted contribution as a percentage of this change gives the percentage of the change due to a change in that cost factor. To take an example quoted by Gold [1, p. 112], between 1899 and 1939 the average selling price of all iron and steel products in the U.S.A. rose by 34.4 per cent. The unit material cost rose by 23 per cent. In 1899 materials constituted 61.2 per cent of total value product. Thus the weighted contribution of material cost increase to price increase was 23 × 0.612 or 14.08 per cent, which is 40.9 per cent of 34.4. Hence the increase in materials costs contributed 40.9 per cent of the increase in average selling price. Similar calculations can be done for the other cost factors, wages and other costs (including profits).

Such an analysis is clearly of great practical use to senior management, enabling them to see in which direction their pressure to reduce costs would be most usefully exercised. Unfortunately, the shorter the time period studied the more difficult it becomes to apply the analysis to any meaningful end.

Taking the whole period studied at Port Talbot, the average selling price rose by 21.2 per cent. Unit costs of materials, wages, salaries, depreciation and other costs (including profits) rose by 26.4, 30.8, 63.9, 33.7 and −1.7 per cent, respectively. In year 1 materials

106

costs constituted 44.9 per cent of total value,[6] wages 16.1 per cent, salaries 4.8 per cent, depreciation 4.9 per cent and other costs 29.3 per cent. Table 6.1 shows the calculation of the contribution of each cost factor to the change in selling price.

Table 6.1. Relative Effects of Cost Adjustments
on Price (years 1-8)

Cost factor	% change years 1-8	Weight year 1	Total contributions	% contribution
Materials	26.4	.449	11.9	56.4
Wages	30.8	.161	5.0	23.7
Salaries	63.9	.048	3.1	14.7
Depreciation	33.7	.049	1.6	7.6
Other	−1.7	.293	−0.5	−2.4
Total		1.000	21.1	100

Cost behaviour at Port Talbot. Let us now examine whether or not the findings at Port Talbot support the beliefs outlined above concerning cost relationships in industry. We have no evidence to support assumption 2, regarding the more effective use of materials (see Fig. 6.5), although the lack of evidence either way is probably a result of the particular period chosen. Production per man-hour has increased, in accordance with assumption 3, and this rise does appear to be largely attributable to technological improvements (see Fig. 6.4). However, there is no evidence to support the hypothesis that this has led to a reduction in the relative importance of wage costs in total product costs. The increase in labour productivity was largely offset by increasing wage rates and Fig. 6.7 shows that the ratio of wages to total costs remained fairly constant throughout the period. Furthermore, we have no evidence to support assumption 4, that the proportion of other costs in average selling price is likely to rise, since the component of other expenses was not disaggregated sufficiently for this purpose.

Figure 6.10 does not give good evidence of "frequent fluctuations in raw material prices, wage rates, profit margins, and levels of production" and again the shortness of the period may be to blame, but it should be noted that in spite of major changes in raw material prices and wage rates, the internal composition of manufacturing costs remained relatively stable, as shown in Fig. 6.7a, contrary to assumption 5. Figure 6.11 does lend some support to assumption 6, that there is an inverse relationship between output and unit costs, although the evidence is not conclusive owing to the major technological changes during the middle of the period.

As for the first and most widely held belief, regarding the large proportion of wage costs in the final price of the product, note the results presented in Fig. 6.7b, where wages averaged 16.9 per cent of selling price, ranging from 16.1 per cent to 18.8 per cent, while wages and salaries together averaged 23 per cent, ranging from 20.9 per cent to 26.5 per cent. This is by no means an insignificant proportion, although it is clearly less than the proportion of material costs and is by no means "the greater part of the selling

[6] Materials constituted over 53 per cent of total unit costs in year 1, but since the effect of changes on price rather than total unit costs is to be examined, it is the proportion of value on turnover which is relevant. The rather low proportion of materials in total costs observed in relation to those found in other studies is partly explained by the fact that in this study some materials were not readily quantified in volume terms and were therefore included in "other expenses".

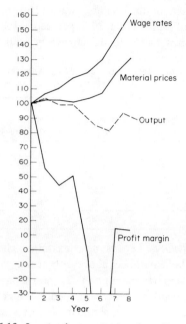

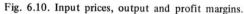

Fig. 6.10. Input prices, output and profit margins.

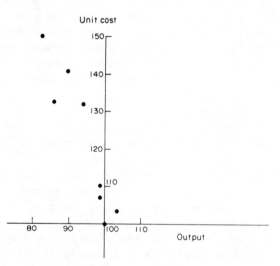

Fig. 6.11. Output vs. total unit costs.

price". That this belief is so widespread is perhaps due to the tendency of managers to regard prices of materials and other expenses as largely fixed and wages as the best target for possible cost cutting. The degree to which this is a reasonable attitude will depend not only on the nature of the operations involved but also on the degree of vertical integration of the particular plant.

In conclusion, findings at Port Talbot do not appear to support some widely held beliefs concerning manufacturing costs and indicate that a very thorough understanding of the nature of the cost structure of a plant is necessary to guide effective managerial decisions concerning cost reduction and performance improvement. It must be stressed again that for the various hypotheses to be properly tested, a longer period of operations would need to be studied in much greater detail.

Managerial Control Ratios

Let us now extend the analysis to cover the range of financial and managerial control ratios suggested in equation (2.4) in Chapter 2. Short-term changes in return on invest-ment are most likely to be due to changes in average selling price, unit costs and capacity utilization, while longer-term trends will be influenced by these three and by changes in the productivity of fixed investment and the allocation of investment, which would not be expected to change dramatically in the short term. Figures 6.12 and 6.13 show that in the case of Port Talbot, unit costs have had a wider amplitude of fluctuations than average prices,[7] but that both moved in the same direction in 5 years out of 8. Costs rose more than price in four of these five, thus reducing unit profits. And in two of the three years when costs and prices moved in opposite directions, both tended to reduce unit profits. Furthermore, Fig. 6.12 suggests that in the short-term unit profit and return on

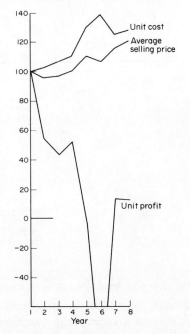

Fig. 6.12. The calculation of unit profit.

[7] It must be remembered that government interference in the setting of prices for steel was present throughout this period, and particularly after nationalization in 1967. This was a major factor in holding down return on capital, particularly during the latter part of the period.

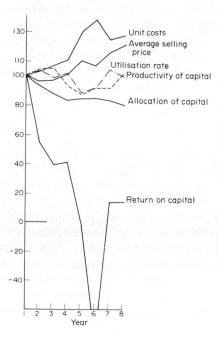

Fig. 6.13. Return on capital and its major components.

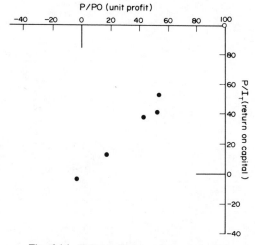

Fig. 6.14. Unit profit vs. return on capital.

capital tend to vary together much more than the other determinants of return on capital, with the corollary that it is changes in unit profit which tend to influence the level of return on capital most strongly. Figure 6.14 shows return on capital plotted against unit profit and the results strongly support the hypothesis that return on capital is linearly correlated with unit profit (the regression coefficient is 0.99). This means that changes in utilization rates tended largely to offset changes in the productivity of net fixed investment as shown in Fig. 6.13, and that the structure of financing (I_F/I_T) was relatively stable.

110

We can now turn to the relationship between the managerial control ratios mentioned above and the financial ratios often used by management. Such financial ratios commonly begin with $Z/I_T \equiv (Z/\text{Sales}) \times (\text{Sales}/I_T)$. But $Z/\text{Sales} \equiv Z/\text{PO} \div (\text{Sales/PO})$ and

$$\frac{\text{Sales}}{\text{Total investment}} \equiv \frac{\text{Output}}{\text{Total investment}} \times \frac{\text{Sales}}{\text{Output}} \; .$$

Hence, one can readily account for changes in profit margin by reference to our findings relating to unit profits and average prices in Fig. 6.12. And the latter is also one of the two determinants of the sales turnover of total investment, yielding the results shown in Fig. 6.15.

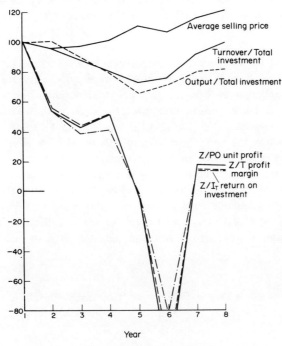

Fig. 6.15. Financial ratios.

Conclusion

In conclusion, the major findings of the Port Talbot study indicate that between years 1 and 8 output fell by some 10.6 per cent, with even sharper declines in year 5 and year 6 when the changeover to BOS steel-making took place. Labour costs also fell steadily and there was an increase in labour productivity. Materials, however, did not decrease until towards the end of the period so that the productivity of materials fell initially. Investment rose sharply in year 4 and year 5, when major expenditure on the BOS plant and harbour took place, and then declined steadily, producing a reverse pattern in the productivity of capital since the investment did not increase capacity. Wage rates, material prices and capital charges all rose, especially wage rates, and total unit costs rose by 41 per cent over the 8-year period. However, individual cost components in total unit costs inflated at

111

varying rates, and the proportion of other expenses rose relative to materials (Figs. 6.7 and 6.9). Return on capital fell dramatically until year 6 (when a loss was made[8]), then rose, although it never reached the level of year 1 again.

Such information can now be used to fulfil the two-fold role of the model, to evaluate performance and plan for the future. In the area of evaluation an obvious question one would like the model to answer is whether or not the massive expenditure of the BOS plant and new harbour was worth while (or is likely to become so). If we take return on capital as a measure of overall performance in the first instance, then year 6 does seem to be a turning-point (see Fig. 6.13). Until the very large expenditure in year 5, return on capital was falling, although it levelled out from years 3 to 4. Whilst no final conclusions can be reached without more data after the investment was made, initial results suggest that without it the plant would have encountered more steeply rising costs and falling profits. This illustrates how the model can provide management with an effective analytical tool for performance evaluation and control, by isolating the major factors that determine changes in the relevant ratios.

It can also be used to plan reactions to possible future changes (as shown in Chapter 4). If, for example, a 20 per cent increase in wage and salary rates is forecast and management wishes to know by how much prices must be raised (assuming that they can be raised) to prevent a fall in profits, then given the data on Port Talbot, total costs and total unit costs will increase by 5 per cent. This means that turnover must increase by 4.2 per cent to produce the same level of profits and without altering output this can only be achieved by a price increase of 1.7 per cent.

Thus, the model can be used both to plan reactions to predicted changes in externally given variables and to assess the effectiveness of past decisions. The relative complexity of operations at Port Talbot and the large number of variables involved have made the model somewhat elaborate, necessitating a great deal of data collection, interpretation and analysis; but this complexity has also shown how necessary it is to build it.

Reference

1. Gold, B. (1971) *Explorations in Managerial Economics.* Macmillan, London; Basic Books, New York.

---

[8] It must be remembered, however, that the size of this loss may have been exaggerated by the way in which the data have been handled (see footnote 3 above) and that at this time government interference in steel price setting was particularly intense.

PART THREE

Further Implications

CHAPTER 7

Reflections on Measurement
and Evaluation

SAMUEL EILON and JUDITH SOESAN

The general problems encountered in the empirical application of the productivity analysis model are discussed at some length in Chapter 3, but it would be appropriate to highlight some of the lessons we have learnt from the case studies described earlier. There were naturally many specific problems during the data-collection stage—largely to do with interpretation, attribution of costs, identification of inputs and outputs, reconciliation of data due to time lags and inventories—these are problems that one normally faces in empirical research and this is where the collaboration of managers of the plants concerned is so invaluable to the research workers. We were very fortunate in this respect.

But apart from these problems, others arose associated with measurement methodology and conventions, and since such problems are not confined to the case studies reported in this book but are of general interest, this chapter is devoted to reviewing them briefly. The major problems discussed here refer to

price and the effect of the base-year
output (or input) index numbers
fixed investment
changes in productivity components
measurement of capacity
the transfer price
analysis of past data

Many of these problems are obviously interlinked and cannot be viewed in isolation, but a discussion of each—coupled with various examples—will help to indicate some of the measurement issues involved.

Price and the Base-year

The first problem that arises in the measurement of outputs or inputs is when product-mix or production methods change to such an extent that not all the products or inputs appear in every annual schedule throughout the study period. Two examples from one of the steel plant case studies are shown in Table 7.1, relating to output from the slabbing mill and from the sinter plant respectively. The first shows that production of

Table 7.1. Two Examples from the Steel Plant

Year	Units	Value	Price per unit
OUTPUTS (tons)			
1. Sinter Plant			
Sinter HP			
1	722,380	4,385,457	6.0708
2	671,312	4,260,731	6.3469
3	700,493	4,105,801	5.8613
4	785,411	4,152,522	5.2671
5	548,896	2,997,360	5.4687
6	–	–	–
7	–	–	–
8	–	–	–
Sinter LP			
1	1,156,453	7,577,726	6.5526
2	1,244,395	8,385,696	6.7388
3	1,446,924	8,573,045	5.9250
4	1,203,561	7,170,415	5.9577
5	1,113,436	6,840,341	6.1435
6	653,041	4,217,429	6.4581
7	1,868,418	12,381,234	6.6266
8	1,626,855	13,333,937	8.1949
2. Slabbing Mill			
Hire rolled			
1	–	–	–
2	–	–	–
3	–	–	–
4	21,360	46,573	2.1804
5	30,739	100,557	3.2713
6	–	–	–
7	–	–	–
8	–	–	–
Mild steel			
1	2,164,523	65,886,373	30.4392
2	2,204,060	71,761,866	32.5589
3	2,118,972	70,269,250	33.1620
4	2,107,622	69,867,866	33.1501
5	1,688,963	60,514,370	35.6293
6	827,478	32,517,112	39.2967
7	1,924,401	73,961,338	38.4334
8	1,869,089	70,195,949	37.5562
Silicon			
1	163,436	6,199,243	37.9307
2	157,335	6,230,690	39.6014
3	133,342	5,455,640	41.1396
4	135,663	5,499,240	40.5360
5	120,084	4,621,765	38.4878
6	27,881	1,257,933	45.1179
7	74,036	3,608,034	48.7335
8	84,133	3,753,173	44.6100

one output (sinter HP) was terminated in the fifth year; the second shows that one product (hire rolled steel) was produced only in the fourth and fifth years.

Turning to the Edgeworth formula for measuring output (see Chapter 3), and assuming year 1 is selected as the base year, we note that the ratio of output PO in year n to the output in base-year 1 is measured by

$$PO_{n,1} = \frac{Q_n(A) \, P(A) + Q_n(B) \, P(B) + \ldots}{Q_1(A) \, P(A) + Q_1(B) \, P(B) + \ldots} \qquad (7.1)$$

Now, the first example in Table 7.1 does not present any problems with respect to the numerator in (7.1), since the physical output in year 6 of sinter HP is 0, its value is 0, irrespective of what price is applied. But in the denominator the output for this product $Q_1(A) \, P(A)$, where with Edgeworth's method

$$P(A) = \tfrac{1}{2}[P_1(A) + P_6(A)]$$

although $P_6(A)$ is not specified. Similarly, in the second example one product is missing from the base-year, so that in the computation of the numerator we need its price $P_1(A)$ for year 1, but this price is not specified.

Such problems can be resolved in a number of ways:

1. *Estimate the unknown prices.* A simple method to adopt for estimating $P_6(A)$ and $P_1(A)$ in the two examples in Table 7.1 is to assume that $P_6(A) = P_1(A)$ in the first and that $P_1(A) = P_4(A)$ in the second. The effect of such a procedure is to value the output of a product in the year in question according to its price in that year, so that with respect to that product no normalization takes place to account for a change in price. This would be particularly inappropriate in cases like Example 1 where a price trend is discernible (in Table 7.1 the "price per unit" is the transfer price, which in this case is equated with the "cost per unit"). To allow the output in years 2, 3, 4 and 5 to be weighted by an average price which is affected by an upward or downward trend, and then in year 6 to revert back to the original price in year 1 clearly creates an anomaly. Admittedly, when the quantities of the products in question are relatively small, compared with the value of the product-mix as a whole, the effect of such a procedure on the result could be small, but the logic behind the method remains suspect none the less.

Another approach is to make estimates for the missing prices based on trend extrapolations, on prevailing market prices for similar products produced by the plant or by competitors, on known prices for the missing products as close as possible to the year in question adjusted by a price index for the industry or by the rate of inflation, and so on. All these methods contain an inevitable element of arbitrariness in defining and estimating the figures involved, although in many cases they prove to be adequate for practical purposes.

2. *Aggregate products.* In Example 1 HP and LP sinter are listed as two separate products. There is sufficient similarity, both in kind and in the unit prices of the two, to allow them to be combined, and in this way the gap for the discontinued product during

117

the latter part of the study period is eliminated.

There are circumstances where such a solution would be undesirable:

when the products are very different in their characteristics and in the market they aim to satisfy;

when they represent activities very dissimilar in terms of added value;

when they belong to entirely different production facilities;

when they command significantly different prices.

In short, aggregation of products helps to solve the technical problems of computations with equation (7.1), but it may prevent us from identifying the very significant issues that would help to explain changes in performance behaviour of various parts of the system.

Effect of the Base-year

In theory, any year can serve as a base-year, although it is generally recommended that it should be as "normal" or "representative" as possible. It must be pointed out, however, that the choice of the base-year may affect the results. Take the example of the outputs of the sinter plant in Table 7.1. If the base-year is selected in turn as year 1, year 2, etc., the calculated output index values are given in Table 7.2. We see, for example, that the output in year 8 is 108.935 when year 1 is taken as a base (column 1), but 111.989 compared with 102.197 when year 2 is taken as a base (column 2). This means that the ratio of outputs between year 8 and year 1 is

$$\frac{108.935}{100} = 1.0893 \text{ according to column 1, but } \frac{111.989}{102.197} = 1.0958 \text{ according to column 2}$$

These inconsistencies persist for the other columns, as demonstrated by the ratio of the two outputs at the bottom of Table 7.2.

Admittedly, in many cases one finds that the discrepancies emanating from the choice of the base-year are very small, and in another example concerning the calculation of output for the coke oven a comparison such as the one given at the end of Table 7.2 revealed only small differences, confined to the third and fourth decimal place. But Table

Table 7.2. Output Index (Edgeworth)

Base-year	1	2	3	4	5	6	7	8
Output for year								
1	100.000	102.197	114.591	105.757	88.890	79.712	103.080	91.798
2	97.850	100.000	112.194	103.426	86.884	77.635	100.478	89.294
3	87.276	89.131	100.000	92.220	77.356	68.622	88.832	78.966
4	94.556	96.687	108.436	100.000	84.169	76.031	98.246	87.574
5	112.498	115.096	129.273	118.809	100.000	90.156	116.675	103.559
6	125.452	128.808	145.725	131.525	110.918	100.000	130.283	113.439
7	97.012	99.524	112.572	101.785	85.708	76.756	100.000	87.071
8	108.935	111.989	126.635	114.189	96.564	88.153	114.848	100.000
Output yr 8 / Output yr 1	1.0893	1.0958	1.1051	1.0797	1.0863	1.1059	1.1142	1.0893

7.2 does demonstrate that serious discrepancies can occur (the difference between columns 4 and 7 in the last row amounts to some 3 per cent), their magnitude being affected by the pattern of price and physical output changes during the period under study.[1]

The reason for such discrepancies lies in the fact that when we examine the structure of equation (7.1) we must conclude that

$$PO_{b,a} \neq PO_{b,c} \, / PO_{c,a}$$

namely, that the output index for year b compared with base-year a is not identical to the ratio of year b compared with c to year c compared with a, although the special case

$$PO_{b,a} PO_{a,b} = 1$$

should be noted, namely that the output of b compared with base-year a is the inverse of the output of a compared with base-year b.

The Output Index Number

The effect of the formulation of the index number should not remain unnoticed. The fundamental problem of measuring output arises from the fact that a single physical measure of product-mix is not possible (except for very special circumstances when simple units of input or capacity may be used as a yardstick), since the different products require different resources for their manufacture. In any given year n, the value of the product-mix may be defined as

$$V_n = Q_n(A) \, P_n(A) + Q_n(B) \, P_n(B) + \ldots$$

so that the output of year b compared with that of year a is simply V_b/V_a, and this has the merit that it is unaffected by the choice of the base-year (indeed, the concept of the base-year does not arise). The shortcoming of such a method of valuation for our purposes is that it fails to measure changes in output when prices change (consider the case where physical outputs remain unchanged but prices increase, this would result in $V_b > V_a$ although no increase in physical output occurs) and a discussion of this issue is to be found in Chapter 3.

A further example to illustrate this point is given in Table 7.3 for a simple two-product case. Assume that in terms of productive capacity the two products A and B require approximately equal resources, so that total output in physical terms is 110, 115 and 120, respectively, for the three years shown in Table 7.3. Due to changing demand, the product-mix is dominated by product B in the first two years but by product A in the third. Six methods for computing the output index are explored: the first method is based on weighting outputs in each year by the prevailing prices in year 1; the second

[1] It should also be realized that the ranking of outputs may be affected by the base year. The example in Table 7.2 shows that while the ranking remains unchanged for most base-years, when we compare base-year 3 and base-year 8 we find that the rankings are as follows:

Base-year 3: 3, 4, 2, 7, 1, 8, 5, 6
Base-year 8: 3, 7, 4, 2, 1, 8, 5, 6

Thus, the choice of the base-year clearly affects the ranking for the output of year 7 in this example.

Table 7.3. An Example of a Two-product Case

| | Quantity | | Price | | Output Index | | | | | |
| | | | | | Computation method† | | | | | |
Year	A	B	A	B	(1)	(2)	(3)	(4)	(5)	(6)
1	10	100	1.0	1.5	100	100	100	100	99.33	117.73
2	20	95	1.0	2.0	101.56	100	102.33	100.68	100	132.19
3	100	20	1.2	1.6	81.25	66.67	88.37	84.94	75.65	100

† *Note on the computation methods:*

			Price	Base-year
Method	(1)		Year 1	1
	(2)		Year 2	1
	(3)		Year 3	1
	(4)		Edgeworth	1
	(5)		Edgeworth	2
	(6)		Edgeworth	3

method relies on prices in year 2 for evaluation, and the third method on prices in year 3; all the three methods use year 1 as the base-year; the last three methods employ the Edgeworth formula, each year taken in turn as the base-year (the fourth method averages prices in the first and second years, and then in the first and third year; the fifth method averages prices in the second year with each of the other, etc.).

The widely divergent results for the output index are noticeable, particularly between the first three methods. Admittedly, this example incorporates a drastic change in product-mix coupled with substantial price differences between the two products, but it serves to demonstrate how the change in output can be affected by the computational procedure employed.

It should be noted that the formulation of the output index proposed by Edgeworth [1] and Fabricant [4] is an approximation for Fisher's Ideal Index [5], which is

$$PO_{n,1} = \sqrt{\frac{Q_n(A)\,P_1(A) + Q_n(B)\,P_1(B) + \ldots}{Q_1(A)\,P_1(A) + Q_1(B)\,P_1(B) + \ldots} \times \frac{Q_n(A)\,P_n(A) + Q_n(B)\,P_n(B) + \ldots}{Q_1(A)\,P_n(A) + Q_1(B)\,P_n(B) + \ldots}} \quad (7.2)$$

The numerator and the denominator of the first fraction value the physical outputs of year n and year 1 (being the base-year), respectively, according to the prices prevailing in year 1, while the numerator and denominator of the second fraction repeat the calculation according to prices in year n.

As an alternative to Edgeworth's formula (7.1), in which the arithmetic mean is used,

$$P(A) = \tfrac{1}{2}[P_1(A) + P_n(A)] \quad (7.3)$$

one can adopt the geometric mean

$$P(A) = \sqrt{P_1(A)\,P_n(A)} \quad (7.4)$$

The example given in Table 7.2 is based on the Edgeworth formula (7.1) and (7.3). When the Fisher Index (7.2) is used instead, or when (7.1) and the approximation (7.4), are used, the results are summarized in Table 7.4, again for each year in turn taken as the base-year. These results show how close the approximation (7.4) brings us to the results of the Fisher Index, closer in fact than the figures in Table 7.2 which is based on the approximation (7.3).

To conclude, the average price mechanism is brought in to ensure that the output index remains unchanged when the product-mix and the physical quantities remain unchanged. However, it still allows the price to affect the output index, as suggested in the example in Table 7.3, and it allows the choice of the base-year to affect the results. In practice this does not usually create serious problems. As for the three variants of the output index discussed here, Fisher's index is cumbersome and is only suitable when all the computations are relegated to a computer, (7.4) is a very good approximation and not too cumbersome to use in practice, while (7.3) is simplest to use and is usually accurate enough.

Table 7.4. Output Index

(a) Fisher's Method

Base year	1	2	3	4	5	6	7	8
Output for year								
1	100.000	102.197	114.583	105.756	88.894	79.730	103.078	91.555
2	97.850	100.000	112.191	103.417	86.887	77.672	100.490	89.090
3	87.273	89.134	100.000	92.215	77.356	68.573	88.763	78.589
4	94.558	96.696	108.442	100.000	84.169	76.011	98.249	87.316
5	112.494	115.092	129.273	118.809	100.000	90.144	116.675	103.323
6	125.424	128.746	145.830	131.559	110.934	100.000	130.283	113.439
7	97.014	99.512	112.660	101.782	85.708	76.756	100.000	87.071
8	109.224	112.246	127.244	114.527	96.783	88.153	114.848	100.000

(b) Approximation (7.4)

1	100.000	102.197	114.584	105.756	88.894	79.745	103.083	91.617
2	97.850	100.000	112.191	103.416	88.887	77.694	100.499	89.161
3	87.272	89.134	100.000	92.212	77.356	68.614	88.789	78.690
4	94.558	96.697	108.446	100.000	84.169	76.015	98.249	87.347
5	112.493	115.092	129.273	118.809	100.000	90.148	116.675	103.359
6	125.399	128.711	145.744	131.553	110.928	100.000	130.283	113.439
7	97.009	99.503	112.627	101.782	85.708	76.756	100.000	87.071
8	109.149	112.156	127.081	114.485	96.750	88.153	114.848	100.000

Note. Approximation (7.3) is used in Table 2.

Fixed Investment

Fixed investment (I_F) is defined as the current net value of investment in fixed capital facilities and it is an important component in determining the productivity of capital within the network of productivity relationships (see Fig. 2.5 and equation (2.4) in Chapter 2). The conventional way to measure fixed investment is by gross fixed investment less depreciation. This means that for a given plant the fixed investment I_F declines with time, so that the ratio of capacity to fixed investment increases (assuming capacity

121

SAMUEL EILON AND JUDITH SOESAN

remains unaffected by the age of the plant), thereby giving the impression of an improvement in the productivity of capital, although no action is specifically taken to increase the amount of capacity per unit of investment.

It is therefore clear that the measurement of fixed investment depends on the accounting procedures adopted in the firm for determining its fixed assets. These procedures may vary from replacement costs of the plant, or reliance on inflation accounting, to gradual write-offs due to depreciation—each will have a significant impact on the computed productivity of capital ratio. Thus, caution must be exercised in the interpretation of trends in this ratio, and particularly when comparison of performance is made for different periods of the same plant or between different plants; unless the measurement of fixed investment is consistent throughout, there is a risk that such comparative studies would be meaningless.

Changes in Profitability Components—The r Model

Gold's model for managerial control ratios, presented in Chapter 2, may be expressed as follows:

$$\frac{\text{Profit}}{\text{Total investment}} = \left(\frac{\text{Product value}}{\text{Output}} - \frac{\text{Total costs}}{\text{Output}}\right)\left(\frac{\text{Output}}{\text{Capacity}}\right)\left(\frac{\text{Capacity}}{\text{Total investment}}\right)$$

$$\text{or } r = (p - c)\, ek \qquad (7.5)$$
$$= aek,$$

where

r = return on total investment = profit/total investment,
p = unit price for the output,
c = unit cost for the output,
a = $p-c$ = unit profit for the output,
e = output/capacity = capacity utilization of the plant,
k = capacity/total investment = $\left(\dfrac{\text{capacity}}{\text{fixed investment}}\right)\left(\dfrac{\text{fixed investment}}{\text{total investment}}\right)$

This is a simplified version of equation (2.4), derived by combining the terms representing the productivity of fixed investment and the internal allocation of investment into a single "k factor", which then expresses the amount of capacity provided per unit of total investment. Equation (7.5), which for the sake of convenience is called *the r model*, reduces the return on total investment r to a dependence on three factors: the unit profit of the output, the capacity utilization of the plant, and the k factor.

If at a given time the rate of return is given by $r = aek$ and if after a certain time period the rate of return becomes $r + \delta r$, it may be expressed as

$$r + \delta r = (a + \delta a)(e + \delta e)(k + \delta k) \qquad (7.6)$$

where δa, δe and δk are the corresponding incremental changes in a, e and k respectively

122

during that period. The difference between (7.6) and (7.5) gives the incremental change δr as follows:

$$\delta r = ek\delta a + ak\delta e + ae\delta k + k\delta a\delta e + a\delta e\delta k + e\delta a\delta k + \delta a\delta e\delta k.$$

If we now divide the left-hand side by r and the right-hand side by aek and substitute the following:

$r^* = \delta r/r$ = change in r relative to the original value of r,
$a^* = \delta a/a$ = change in a relative to the original value of a,
$e^* = \delta e/e$ = change in e relative to the original value of e,
$k^* = \delta k/k$ = change in k relative to the original value of k,

we get (similar to [2]):

$$r^* = a^* + e^* + k^* + a^*e^* + e^*k^* + k^*a^* + a^*e^*k^*. \tag{7.7}$$

Where the relative changes of a^*, e^* and k^* are small (say, below 0.1) then the last four terms in (7.7) may be ignored, reducing (7.7) to

$$r^* = a^* + e^* + k^* . \tag{7.8}$$

Equations (7.7) and (7.8) indicate how a relative change in rate of return can be attributed to relative changes in the three factors in question and to the interactions between them. When (7.8) holds, the overall relative change in r is the sum of the relative changes in a, e and k. The last four terms in (7.7) represent residuals due to the combined effect of these factors, over and above their identified individual effects (the interactions of all three factors given by the last term in (7.7) is of a third-order effect). Thus, if we want to identify the total effect of a change in a, then from (7.7) it would be (ignoring the last term $a^*e^*k^*$)

$$a^* (1 + e^* + k^*) .$$

The first term here describes the direct contribution of a^*, the second term in the brackets represents the relative effect of the interaction of e^* on this contribution, and the third term is the relative effect of k^*. In special cases, simpler expressions are obtained. For example, when e and k remain constant over a period of time we find that $r^* = a^*$, namely the change in the rate of return is entirely attributable to a change in the unit profit.

It must be emphasized here that equation (7.7) does not identify the *original cause or causes* that subsequently lead to a series of changes in the system and thereby to changes in the values of the three components, a, e and k; it merely provides a decomposition of the relative change in the rate of return into its several constituent parts, so that their relative contributions can be better appreciated.

One example of how this model can be used relates to the case study in Chapter 4, where Table 4.4 depicts the expected effect of certain forecasts regarding the possible increases in demand, in wage rates and the price of electricity. The calculations revealed

123

that if the price of the output is to remain unchanged, the return on investment would decline by 11.6 per cent from 100 to 88.4, or $r^* = -0.116$. Using equation (7.8)

$$r^* = a^* + e^* + k^*$$

which in this case yields (assuming no change in the k factor)

$$-0.116 = -0.127 + 0.013 + 0.$$

In this case the approximation (7.8) is adequate; the discrepancy of 0.002 is accounted for by a^*e^* in equation (7.7).

Another example is the use of the r model in the analysis of change in return on investment for the whole plant in the case study described in Chapter 6. To proceed with the decomposition of r^* we first assemble the basic data in Table 7.5, where values for r, a, e and k are given. From these values we can readily compute the relative changes that occurred; for example, in comparing year 2 with year 1 the value of r^* is

$$r^* = \frac{r_2 - r_1}{r_1} = \frac{55.6 - 100}{100} = -.444$$

and similarly the values for the relative changes a^*, e^* and k^* can be computed. The decomposition of r^* is thus shown in detail in Table 7.6.

Table 7.5. Values for Return on Investment and its
Components (all figures compared with base year 1)

Year	r (Z/I_T)	a (Z/PO)	e (PO/CAP)	k (CAP/I_T)
1	100	100	100	100
2	55.6	55.4	103.4	96.9
3	46.2	51.3	98.5	91.4
4	43.0	54.2	101.8	78.0
5	7.7	11.8	88.4	73.9
6	-57.5	-81.0	91.5	77.5
7	28.5	35.8	104.3	76.2
8	18.1	22.2	99.3	82.4

Table 7.6. Components in the Relative Change in Return on Investment (r^*)

Comparison of year	r^*	a^*	e^*	k^*	a^*e^*	e^*k^*	k^*a^*
2 vs. 1	-.444	-.446	.034	-.031	-.015	-.001	.014
3 vs. 2	-.169	-.076	-.047	-.057	.004	.003	.004
4 vs. 3	-.069	.057	.033	-.147	.002	-.005	-.008
5 vs. 4	-.821	-.782	-.132	-.053	.103	.007	.041
8 vs. 7	-.365	-.380	-.048	.081	.018	-.004	-.031
8 vs. 1	-.819	-.778	-.068	-.176	.053	.012	.137

We find that in all cases the decomposition given in equation (7.7)–and ignoring the last term–is a very good approximation, and even with the lapse of a considerable time interval, when the last year of the study period is compared with the base-year (see the last row in Table 7.6) with a substantial change in the return on investment, the sum of the six components in equation (7.7) accounts very closely for the value of r^* (the relatively small discrepancy can be eliminated by the seventh term in (7.7)). We further find that in most cases in Table 7.6 the component a^* is dominant, that compared with other effects the relative changes in plant utilization (column e^*) are small, that (as expected) the major change in k^* coincides with capital investment taking place in year 4. Thus, Table 7.6 reinforces the analyses described earlier and summarizes information of interest to the manager in highlighting where major adjustments occur year by year.

On Measuring Capacity and Utilization

The problem of measuring capacity is discussed in some detail by Gold in Chapter 3 (see also [6]), stating the view that (under certain conditions) reasonable acceptable estimates of practical capacity can be made, largely based on management's estimate (however crude) of the productive capacity which it administers.

It should be pointed out that one of the requirements for measuring capacity is that an adequate supply is available of labour, materials and other inputs needed to attain the productive potential of given capital facilities. Such an assumption is generally considered reasonable in the case of studies limited to individual plants and firms, but less tenable for wider sectors of the economy, because simultaneous increases in demand for resources from many quarters may exceed the currently available supply. In such instances, output potentials must be reconsidered in terms of the availability of the relevant input factors.

Even at the plant or departmental level the determination of capacity is subject to interpretation and problems of measurement. Take, for example, the special case of a single product routed through a series of machines in a plant; the capacity of each machine may be defined as *the maximum physical quantity that can be processed during a time interval at given operating conditions*, and the capacity of the whole plant would then be determined by the "bottleneck", namely by the lowest rate of production along the sequence.

Such a definition assumes that agreement can be reached as to what is meant by "given operating conditions", and indeed that such conditions remain static. But changes in these conditions may well occur. It may be possible, for example, to speed up the rate of production of the constraining machine (and thereby increase the capacity of the plant as a whole), perhaps at the expense of a higher rate of wear of the machine, or by involving higher maintenance costs. The rate of production may even depend at times on the quality and the cost of the input, and in turn it may affect the quality of the output. Thus, there could be several possible "states" of operating conditions, each state corresponding to a certain machine or plant capacity, and this may occur even in the relatively simple one-product case.

Consider now the multi-product plant and the question of what is precisely meant by the capacity of this plant [3]. Presumably, it is the set of all product-mixes that the designer and the plant manager expect the plant to produce per unit time, given the availability of material, labour and whatever other inputs are necessary. In a labour-dominated process such a definition is obviously not adequate, since capacity is then entirely dependent on the manpower level. Even in a capital dominated process, capacity will depend on various factors, as mentioned earlier, such as the number of shifts worked, perhaps even on the quality of raw materials. In principle, therefore, the set of all product-mixes for given operating conditions may be determined in the form of a production-possibilities curve, or a full-capacity envelope as interpreted in linear or non-linear programming models through a series of constraints, provided these constraints can be defined and measured consistently and unambiguously.

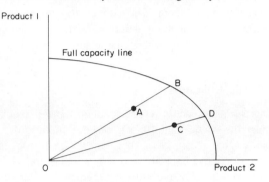

Fig. 7.1. Plant utilization.

If the full capacity envelope can be determined, then the ratio e for plant utilization (output/capacity) defined earlier is simply found as shown in Fig. 7.1, which—for simplicity of illustration—is confined to a two-product case: point A is a given level of operation; the extension of OA cuts the full capacity envelope at point B, and as any point on this line (including B) has a product-mix in the same proportions as at A, the plant utilization e may be measured by OA/OB. This method will apply to any product-mix, so that if the plant in one period operates at point A and in another period at point C the relative performance in terms of plant utilization can be regarded as a change from $e_1 = $ OA/OB to $e_2 = $ OC/OD. There is in principle no conceptual difficulty in extending this method to any number of products.

Thus, plant utilization can be measured when the full-capacity envelope is known, even when changes in product-mix occur. It should be noted that the measurement of *output* on its own presents the additional difficulty of comparing one product-mix with another. The reduction of all the products in the mix to a single common denominator can be done through price factors, as mentioned earlier, so that output is measured not in physical terms but by the weighted value of the products produced (with appropriate adjustments to account for price changes from period to period, as discussed earlier in this chapter and in Chapter 2).

The measurement of physical output without resorting to the use of the price factor may therefore only be done by reference to plant utilization. Thus, if output in two successive periods in Fig. 7.1 is represented by product-mixes A and C respectively, corresponding plant utilization values being e_1 and e_2, then we may assert that physical output in period 2 is higher than in period 1 if $e_2 > e_1$, and furthermore that the increase may be measured by e_2/e_1. This method allows output to be measured in *relative* terms, unlike measurement of the monetary value of the products which yields quantities in

126

absolute terms (subject to the necessary adjustment of price from one period to another). It is, of course, possible that in the example shown in Fig. 7.1 one method will suggest that output has increased from point A to point C, whereas the other that it has decreased, and this illustrates how vital it is in any study to be consistent in the definition and application of measuring tools.

The Case of Intermediate Outputs

A special problem may arise when some of the output of an intermediate process is available for sale, as in the case of the production of coke in the iron-making department described in Chapter 5. The major part of the produced coke is used as an input to the blast furnace, but some excess production is sold.

A simple example of such a case is described schematically in Fig. 7.2, where process

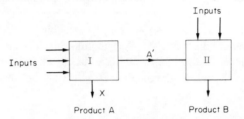

Fig. 7.2. Two products from two inter-department processes.

(or department) I produces product A, of which a quantity A' goes into process (or department) II and an excess amount X is sold, so that the total production of I is

$$A = A' + X \leqslant A_{max}$$

and the production level A cannot exceed the maximum capacity of process I given by the upper limit A_{max}. Now, process II has a capacity defined by B_{max}, and in the special case when the two processes are in balance the whole of the output A_{max} will be needed as an input to process II to product B_{max}. This is shown in Fig. 7.3, where a lower limit B_{min} is imposed on process II for technical reasons, so that process II is similarly constrained and is required to produce at least A_{min} as an input to II.

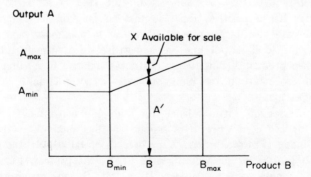

Fig. 7.3. Capacities with processes I and II in balance.

127

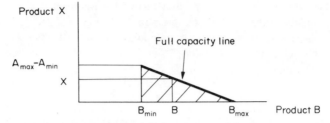

Fig. 7.4. The capacity line for the two-product mix in Fig. 7.3.

If we now regard the two-machine complex as a single entity producing two products for sale, namely X and B, the full-capacity line (or the production possibilities curve) for the two-product mix is shown in Fig. 7.4, where the shaded area represents all the possible combinations of output of X and B. Provided product X is profitable (i.e. it is not sold below cost), it would be advantageous—for any given level of B—to operate process I at full capacity, so that the excess X available for sale will vary from 0 to $A_{max}-A_{min}$, depending on the value of B. The full-capacity line therefore is the set of all possible product-mixes X and B that can be produced with the given capacity constraints on processes I and II, given that B must lie between the limits B_{min} and B_{max}.

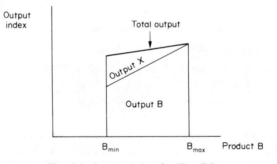

Fig. 7.5. Output index for Fig. 7.4.

If the total output of this product-mix is to be expressed in terms of value through the use of an output index, the result would be as shown in Fig. 7.5 (linear relationships were assumed here and in Figs. 7.3 and 7.4 for the sake of simplicity). Notice that the total output index has a positive slope, so that to maximize the value of the output, efforts should be made to operate process II as near to maximum capacity as possible. If, for some reason, the total output line has a negative slope, namely total output declines as B increases, then product X must be so profitable (relative to B) that there would be a tendency to run process II at its minimum level, or even close it down, to allow the output of X to increase.

If the two processes are not in balance, for example when process I has spare capacity to produce X_0 for sale even when II is supplied at the maximum, then Fig. 7.4 applies and the output index is shown in Fig. 7.7, where the total output line is shifted upwards (compared with Fig. 7.5) by the output value of X_0 that process I can produce for sale after meeting the requirements of process II in full. On the assumption that process I operates at full capacity, the total output index depends here entirely on the level of

128

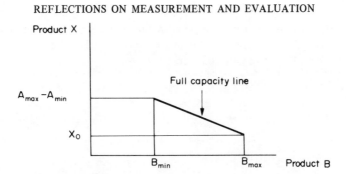

Fig. 7.6. The capacity line when two processes are not in balance.

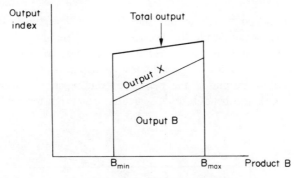

Fig. 7.7. Output index for Fig. 7.6.

output of product B (whether processes I and II are in balance or not), namely on the level of utilization of process II.

Effect of Transfer Price

When departments in a plant are linked in series, with the output of one becoming the input to another, the computed profitability of each department depends on the transfer pricing system adopted. In the example in Fig. 7.2 the total output of department I is A, of which X is sold, say, at s per unit and A' is transferred at a price of t per unit. In the special case where $X=0$, the value of the output of I is solely dependent on the transfer price t, and as t increases so does the unit profit of I increase, while the unit profit of II declines.

One extreme policy for the transfer price is to fix it at cost, as in the example of the iron-making and steel-making departments in the case studies in Chapter 5. As we have seen, this means that no profitability analysis for the supplying departments can be carried out and their economic performance is then confined to the examination of their unit cost structure. Since all the profit in that case is attributed to the final department in the plant, the profitability of that department can be grossly distorted; this is particularly important when its performance is to be compared with similar departments in other plants, where other methods for transfer pricing are in operation and where seemingly different levels of performance can be ascertained.

The effect of the transfer price on the return on investment in department I in Fig. 7.2 is clear from equation (7.5). If the department operates at full capacity, and if k is

129

assumed constant, then the return r depends on the unit profit a, which (for a given level of unit costs) depends entirely on the unit price p. The value of the output of department I is $sX + tA'$, so that the unit cost is

$$p = \frac{sX + tA'}{A}$$

$$= s(1-u) + tu$$

$$= s\left[1 - u\left(1 - \frac{t}{s}\right)\right]$$

where $u = A'/A$ = proportion of the output transferred to department II. Clearly, then, p increases with the price s and, with the transfer price t, but decreases with u as long as $s > t$: for any given value of s the unit price p increases with t/s, and for any given value of the latter (provided $t/s < 1$) it is in the interest of department I to decrease u (see Fig. 7.8), namely to divert its output to the market at the expense of supplying department II. However, when $t/s > 1$ the benefit to I is greater from transfer to II and it will then attempt to increase u.

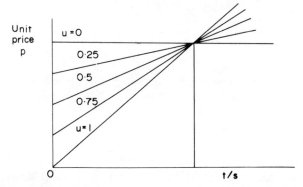

Fig. 7.8. Effect of t/s and u on unit price for a supplier department.

The transfer price affects department II in the opposite way, although the effect is muted by the prices of its other inputs, and it is therefore possible for a change in t to have a seemingly greater influence on the profitability of I than on that of II. The transfer price has, of course, no computation effect on the profitability of the whole plant, since it is the cost of material inputs from the outside and not on internal transfers that such computation of unit profit is based; the effect, if any, is related to the way the transfer price serves to motivate individual sections of the plant, and thereby influence their performance.

Analysis of Past Data

The case studies described in Chapters 4-6 are largely concerned with the analysis of past data. The cost model in Fig. 2.3 and the managerial control ratios in Fig. 2.5 were used to determine the major causes for changes in the level of performance of a plant, or

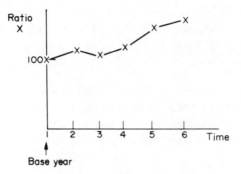

Fig. 7.9. Time-based record.

of its component parts, and to trace the effects that particular managerial decisions or changes in the inputs have had on certain performance criteria.

Such analyses of past data usually resort to the following three methodological tools:

(a) *Time-based analysis*—a record of a given parameter or ratio X is plotted over a period of time, as shown in Fig. 7.9, to reveal any exceptional modes of behaviour. This allows a stationary pattern or upward/downward trends to be detected, as well as peaks and troughs, so that the reasons for their occurrence may then be sought. Trends are often due to gradual changes in market demand or to inflationary effects, while exceptional peaks and troughs may at times be traced to capital expenditure, to opening or closing production facilities, or to drastic changes in product-mix, in material inputs, or in prices. A series of time-based records of various ratios either in absolute terms, or relative to the base year, which is taken as 100 as shown in Fig. 7.9 (the base-year is usually identified as the beginning of the period under study) may provide a pattern of behaviour for the system and its component parts, and for the underlying background of events that influence this behaviour. This type of analysis was used extensively in the various case studies described in Chapters 4-6.

(b) *A pattern analysis*—a time-based record, such as the one shown in Fig. 7.9, depicts the changes of a single parameter or ratio with time. One way to find whether the trends for two ratios are similar is to superimpose their time-based records on each other. This would show, for example, whether both have similar or opposite trends, or whether peaks

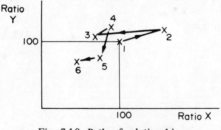

Fig. 7.10. Path of relationship.

and troughs occur at the same time. Another method is to plot one ratio against the other as shown in Fig. 7.10, where the numerals denote the time periods corresponding to the values of X and Y (again, it is often convenient to express values relative to the base-year 1, where the base value is taken as 100). In this way, a time-path of the relationship between X and Y is established and some inferences may be drawn from the pattern that emerges. In the example in Fig. 7.10 one could note the fact that in every single case an increase or decrease in X was accompanied by a corresponding increase or decrease in Y. In certain cases a *hysteresis effect* may be detected, such as in the example in Fig. 7.11, where again increases or decreases of X and Y go together, but when X increases and then declines it leaves Y with a residual effect, so that Y has the tendency not to return to its original value when X does. This hysteresis effect is often due to irreversible processes in economics, for example in the case of inflation or when wage rates tend to go up and rarely come down.

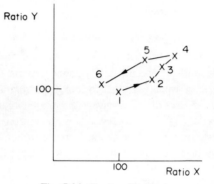

Fig. 7.11. Hysteresis effect.

(c) *Regression analysis*—here the time-path of Fig. 7.10 is ignored and the values are plotted as shown in Fig. 7.12. The order in which they are generated in history is thought to be of minor significance, and the major purpose is to discover whether the two variables X and Y are closely associated with each other (the most commonly used relationship is that of linear regression, as shown in Fig. 7.12). Once the hypothesis of a direct relationship between the two variables is held (the goodness of such a hypothesis is indicated by the value of the regression coefficient), the investigator may pursue questions of causality or embark on more elaborate analyses, such as non-linear and/or multiple-regressions. This type of analysis was not used a great deal in the studies described in Chapters 4-6, largely because of the short series of data collected, particularly in the case of the major studies in Chapter 5. The fewer the number of observations available the less

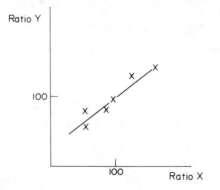

Fig. 7.12. Regression of Y against X.

132

the confidence one can place in the accuracy of the regression coefficient. However, examples of its use can be found in Chapter 6 where the relationships between return on capital and unit profit and between output and various unit costs are discussed.

References

1. Edgeworth, F. Y. (1925) The plurality of index numbers. *Economic Journal*, vol. 35, pp. 379-88.
2. Eilon, S. (1975) Changes in profitability components. *Omega*, vol. 3, no. 3, pp. 353-4.
3. Eilon, S. and Teague, J. (1973) On measures of productivity. *Omega,* vol. 1, no. 4, pp. 505-11.
4. Fabricant, S. (1940) *Output of Manufacturing Industries 1899-1937.* National Bureau of Economic Research, New York.
5. Fisher, I. (1922) *The Making of Index Numbers.* Houghton Mifflin Co., Boston and New York.
6. Gold, B. (1971) *Explorations in Managerial Economics.* Macmillan, London.

CHAPTER 8

Prediction and Planning

SAMUEL EILON and JUDITH SOESAN

We reviewed in the previous chapter some of the methods used for the analysis of past operations. Having constructed a model based on historical data to explain past behaviour of the system and its performance criteria, the manager may wish to turn to the predictive use of the model and pose questions about the expected response of the system to certain changes that may occur. Some of these changes may be imposed on the system by outside factors, some may be the result of management decisions which the manager of the plant is in a position to control or influence. The model may help to give indications, or to provide explicit predictions, as to how the system is likely to behave in the future under given conditions.

Three major methods of analysis may be used for the purpose and these will be briefly reviewed in this chapter: (a) the method of sensitivity analysis, (b) a deterministic analysis for a given set of circumstances, and (c) a risk simulation approach. It should be emphasized at the outset that these are not mutually exclusive tools; each has a contribution to make and situations often arise where all three are useful to employ.

Sensitivity Analysis

A complete model, such as the one depicted in Fig. 2.5, involves many variables and inter-relationships. Inevitably, some variables are likely to be more significant than others, and the purpose of sensitivity analysis is to establish the extent to which various criteria, as well as the system as a whole, are affected by a given incremental change of each variable. Thus, a *sensitivity table* may be constructed, such as in Table 8.1, where for an incremental change of 1.0 per cent for each of the factors listed on the left the possible effect (in per cent) is recorded for each of the ratios enumerated at the top of the table. In some cases the effect would be quite minimal, in others the relative impact could be significant; and this is precisely the purpose of the table, to identify the most important variables in the performance model. The table contains the major factors and ratios that are likely to be of interest (see equation (2.4)), but it is not intended as a comprehensive list and clearly the table would need to be modified to suit *ad hoc* needs. Note that an increase in some of the factors on the left would have an adverse effect on some of the ratios listed (for example, an increase in unit cost will reduce the unit profit margin) and this will be entered in the appropriate cell with a negative sign. It is often possible to entertain the assumption that the incremental changes are relatively small and that a

Table 8.1. An Incremental Sensitivity Table

1% change in	Effect on (in per cent)							
	Output unit cost				Unit profit margin $a*$	Output / Capacity $e*$	Capacity / Total inv. $k*$	Return on inv. $r*$
	Labour	Materials	Capital	Total				
Labour { M-hr/output unit								
Wage rates								
Materials { Volume/output unit								
Av. costs								
Av. unit costs								
Fixed inv.								
Capacity								
Output								
Sale price								

decremental change in any of the factors listed on the left will result in the same magnitude of change, but with the opposite sign, in each of the ratios at the top. This assumption implies reversibility, namely the proposition that incremental and decremental changes have the same absolute effects (but in opposite directions) independent of previous changes, and as an approximation such an assumption is usually acceptable for practical purposes, particularly when the changes are relatively small. The last four columns relate to the incremental relative changes of the unit profit, the plant utilization and the k factor, discussed earlier in equation (7.5).

Table 8.2. An Incremental Sensitivity Table for a Steel Plant (for a 1 per cent rise in certain variables)

	Output unit cost				Unit profit margin $a*$	Output / Capacity $e*$	Capacity / Total inv. $k*$	Return on inv.† $r*$
	Labour	Materials	Capital	Total				
Labour { M-hr/output unit	1	0	0	0.104	−0.536	0	0	−0.536
Wage rates	1	0	0	0.104	−0.536	0	0	−0.536
Materials { Volume/output unit	0	1	0	0.534	−2.750	0	0	−2.750
Av. costs	0	1	0	0.534	−2.750	0	0	−2.750
Av. unit costs	0.104	0.534	0.059	1	−5.150	0	0	−5.150
Fixed inv.	0	0	1	0.059	−0.304	0	−0.961	−1.262
Capacity	0	0	0	0	0	−0.990	1	0
Output	−0.990	−0.990	−0.990	−0.990	−0.990††	1	0	0
Sale price	0	0	0	0	6.150	0	0	6.150

† Taking account of equation (7.7).
†† Assuming total revenue remains unchanged.

Table 8.3. An Incremental Sensitivity Table for a Steel Plant (for a 1 per cent fall in certain variables)†

		Output unit cost			Unit profit margin $a*$	Output Capacity $e*$	Capacity Total inv. $k*$	Return on inv. $r*$
		Labour	Materials	Capital	Total				
Labour {	M-hr/output unit	−1	0	0	−0.104	0.536	0	0	0.536
	Wage rates	−1	0	0	−0.104	0.536	0	0	0.536
Materials {	Volume/output unit	0	−1	0	−0.534	2.750	0	0	2.750
	Av. costs	0	−1	0	−0.534	2.750	0	0	2.750
Av. unit costs		−0.104	−0.534	−0.059	−1	5.150	0	0	5.150
Fixed inv.		0	0	−1	−0.059	0.304	0	0.979	1.286
Capacity		0	0	0	0	0	1.010	−1	0
Output		1.010	1.010	1.010	1.010	1.010†	−1	0	0
Sale price		0	0	0	0	−6.150	0	0	−6.150

† See footnotes for Table 8.2.

Examples of the use of this sensitivity table are shown in Tables 8.2 and 8.3, which were constructed for the Port Talbot plant, following the case study in Chapter 6.

The assumptions contained within the tables are:

(i)   that whilst the factor listed on the left changes, all other factors remain constant;

(ii) that the base-year cost proportions, profit to turnover margin and the ratio of fixed to total investment are constant throughout at the levels operating in the base-year;

(iii) that a 1 per cent change in fixed investment in either direction alters capital charges by 1 per cent in the same direction;

(iv) that a 1 per cent increase in capacity results from some change (e.g. rescheduling, alteration in production-mix) other than a change in fixed investment and has no effect on unit labour or material costs; and that a 1 per cent fall in capacity is the result of the closure of investment which has been fully written off and therefore has no effect on capital or other unit costs.

The two tables, one for a rise and the other for a fall of 1 per cent in each variable, are shown in order to draw attention to the asymmetry of effect of changes in fixed investment, capacity and output, since this asymmetry is embedded in the model, although the differences between the absolute values in the two tables in this case are relatively small. We notice here the significant effect on return on investment exercised by the sale price and by the total unit cost (1 per cent increase resulting in an expected 6.15 per cent increase and 5.15 per cent decline respectively in the return on investment), contrasted by the relatively low effect of changes in capacity and the level of output. Within the total unit cost we find that materials costs are most significant (with 1 per cent increase yielding a decline of 2.75 per cent in the return on investment) while labour unit costs have a lower effect (an increment of 1 per cent leading to a decline of about ½ per cent in the return).

It should be emphasized that the incremental sensitivity table is strictly valid only at a given level of operations, usually identified as the current plant activity. Like the concept of marginal costing, the sensitivity table depicts marginal values. If a 10 per cent increase in any given parameter takes place, the results will not necessarily be ten times the values shown in the table. Nor do these values predict the incremental changes that would occur if the mode of operation of the plant and the values of the major variables are significantly different from those assumed when the table is constructed. These are important limitations; nevertheless, the incremental sensitivity table is a very useful tool for the purpose of managerial control and it provides a simple synoptic picture which highlights the most significant components in the model for any given situation.

Deterministic Appraisal

In Table 8.1 it is assumed that an incremental change takes place for each of the listed factors in isolation. The manager may be interested in exploring the possible effect of several changes taking place simultaneously, such as 10 per cent increase in average wage rates, 5 per cent increase in certain material costs and 1 per cent increase in the unit sales price. Because of the intricate relationships between the many factors involved, it is not appropriate simply to add the corresponding effects from Table 8.1 (e.g. the combined effect of 1 per cent increase in materials costs and 1 per cent increase in output is not necessarily the same as the sum of the two separate effects). Thus, an *ad hoc* analysis needs to be undertaken for an assumed specified set of changes to trace their combined effects on the various components of the model. Such a set of assumptions constitutes a given scenario, and the deterministic appraisal exercise addresses itself to that particular scenario.

It should be noted that the incremental sensitivity table is a special case of the deterministic appraisal method, with each row in the table representing the computational results of one such appraisal.

An example of the use of a deterministic appraisal for a given set of future estimates is given in Chapter 4, where the effect of simultaneous increases in demand, in the wage rate and in the price of electricity (10, 5 and 10 per cent, respectively) is explored. The results are shown in Table 4.4, where the effects of these combined increases are listed for indices of physical inputs and outputs, for unit cost, and for the various cost proportions; the adverse effects on profit and on return on investment are also computed. Table 4.4 then proceeds to show that the return on investment can be maintained if the price of the marginal output is allowed to increase by 70 per cent, noting again the consequent effect this is likely to have on unit cost and its constituent components.

Thus, various alternative scenarios may be explored through a series of deterministic appraisals, giving the manager a reasonably good insight into the behaviour of the system under his control. Armed with information about the possible consequences of changes in the various parameters that are involved, he may be in a better position to anticipate the results and to take corrective action, as and when appropriate.

Risk Simulation

The two methods of analysis described earlier are deterministic, since both rely on single estimates for each of the variables listed on the left in Table 8.1 (or other pertinent variables)—the sensitivity table attempts to delineate the effects of a change in

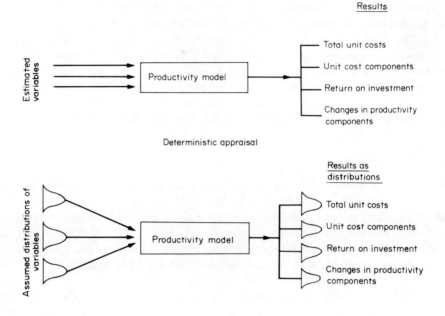

Fig. 8.1. The methods of deterministic appraisal and risk simulation.

each variable, while the deterministic appraisal method explores the effects of simultaneous changes in several variables. In both cases it is assumed that the changes in question are known precisely in advance.

There are, however, many circumstances where the possible changes would be specified by ranges of values, rather than by single estimates (see Fig. 8.1). For example, based on his intimate knowledge of the environment in which he operates, a manager may be able to state that during the forthcoming year labour wage rates are likely to increase between 5 and 10 per cent, that materials costs will rise between 2 and 6 per cent, that demand would increase between 4 and 8 per cent and that price will increase by 5 per cent. Here, only for the last variable a single estimate is given, whereas the values for the others need to be sampled from distributions lying within the ranges specified. This is equivalent to repeating the deterministic analysis many times over, each time for the set of variables sampled from the ranges, and each time computing the effects on any of the required relevant ratios, such as those shown at the top of Table 8.1. In this way, it is not a single estimate for, say, the effect on the return on investment that is found, but a distribution of values of the return on investment; from such a distribution, the expected value and the range within which the resultant value would lie (with certain confidence limits) can then be readily computed (see Fig. 8.1). Details about the risk simulation technique, and the various sampling methods that may be employed for generating sets of estimates for computational purposes, are given by Eilon and Fowkes [1].

To illustrate the use of the deterministic appraisal and the risk simulation methods, we may cite the example of the slab mill in the steel plant, described in Chapter 5. Data for the slab mill, all related to the base-year, are given in Table 8.4. Suppose that estimates

Table 8.4. Base-year Data for a Slab Mill

	Quantity	Unit cost (£)	Cost (£,000)
Outputs			
Mild steel slabs (tons)	2,158,750	31.82	68,691
Silicon slabs (tons)	169,459	35.76	6060
Hire rolled slabs (tons)	0	2.87	0
Scrap (tons)	268,789	9.88	2656
Materials			
Mild steel ingots (tons)	2,407,975	26.95	64,895
Silicon ingots (tons)	189,023	30.49	5763
Hire rolled ingots (tons)	0	1.00	0
Expenses			
Fuels, etc.			987
Labour			
Maintenance (hours)	432,297	0.56	242
Production (hours)	779,405	0.63	491
Depreciation charges			522

Cost proportions	
Materials	0.9437
Labour	0.0096
Capital	0.0068
Other	0.0403

are then made that total man-hours are likely to increase by 0-15 per cent and wage rates by 5-15 per cent, coupled with certain changes in outputs and price. What would the effect of these changes be on the unit cost structure on the slab mill?

The assumed possible changes in the base year data are summarized in Table 8.5: the first column lists the variables subject to change, the second gives single value estimates for the level of change in each variable, and the third column shows each estimate as a range with a mean, which in almost all cases is the same as the single estimate given in the second column. On reasonable assumptions concerning scrap ratios and changes in fuel costs, the following analyses were then carried out:

(1) A deterministic appraisal based on the estimates in the second column in Table 8.5.

(2) A risk simulation based on the range estimates in the third column in Table 8.5.

The objectives of the analyses were two-fold: first, to forecast the effects of the estimated changes on total unit costs and on return on investment, and secondly to estimate the price that should be charged for slabs in order to ensure that there is a chance of about 1:5 that return on investment would not decline (i.e. giving a probability of about 16.6 per cent against a decline).

The risk simulation exercise was based on the CIA program[1] with discriminate

[1] CIA (Capital Investment Appraisal) program, London University Computing Services, developed by Eilon, S. and Tilley, R. P. R. (1973).

sampling, where the following relationships were assumed:[2]

A positive correlation between the first two products in Table 8.5 (a high output of the first is accompanied by a high output of the second, similarly low outputs go together).

A negative correlation between each of these two outputs and its cost (high output tends to be associated with low cost and vice versa).

A negative correlation between man-hours and the wage rate.

The method of discriminate sampling ensures that such relationships are accounted for in the series of sampled data fed into the model. Where it is not necessary to maintain particular relationships between the variables, the procedure of independent sampling is resorted to, namely each variable is sampled from its own distribution, irrespective of the values of other sampled variables [1].

Table 8.5. Assumed Changes in Base-year Slab Mill Data

Variable	Single estimates for DA (deterministic appraisal)	Range estimates for RS (risk simulation)
Labour		
Total man-hours	down 5%	down 0-10% mean 5%
Wage rates	up 10%	up 5-15% mean 10%
Outputs		
(1) Mild steel slabs	up 10%	up 5-15% mean 10%
(2) Silicon slabs	down 5%	down 0-10% mean 5%
(3) Hire rolled slabs	0	0 or between 25,089 and 35,478[3]
Costs		
Hire rolled ingots	£1.00	£0.9171-£1.1702 mean £1.0436
Mild steel and silicon ingots	up 5%	up 0-10% mean 5%

Table 8.6. Increases in Unit Cost and its Components (in per cent) by DA (deterministic appraisal) and RS (risk simulation)

Increases in unit costs	$\Delta\left(\dfrac{TC}{PO}\right)$ (total)	$\Delta\left(\dfrac{M}{PO}\right)$ (materials)	$\Delta\left(\dfrac{W}{PO}\right)$ (wages)	$\Delta\left(\dfrac{CC}{PO}\right)$ (capital)	$\Delta\left(\dfrac{OE}{PO}\right)$ (other expenses)
DA	4.2	4.9	−4.0	−8.1	−8.1
RS−mean	4.2	4.8	−3.1	−7.2	−7.2
(st. dev.)	(2.2)	(2.3)	(1.8)	(1.3)	(1.3)

The results of the deterministic appraisal method and of the risk simulation (consisting of 1000 runs) for the increase in unit cost and its components are shown in Table 8.6, the analysis for each cost component being based on the following relationship (referred to in Chapters 2 and 5):

[2] These assumptions were derived from an analysis of the original data.

[3] The distribution in the model varies from 0 to 35,478 with a mean of 25,089. If a value below the mean is selected it is set to 0. The reason for this is that small batches of rolling of this output are not undertaken by the plant.

$$\Delta\left(\frac{TC}{PO}\right)_{2,1} = \Delta\left(\frac{M}{PO}\right)_{2,1}\left(\frac{M}{TC}\right)_1 + \Delta\left(\frac{W}{PO}\right)_{2,1}\left(\frac{W}{TC}\right)_1 + \Delta\left(\frac{CC}{PO}\right)_{2,1}\left(\frac{CC}{TC}\right)_1 + \Delta\left(\frac{OE}{PO}\right)_{2,1}\left(\frac{OE}{TC}\right)_1$$

where $\Delta(TC/PO)_{2,1}$ is the relative change in total unit costs (compared with year 1) and $(M/TC)_1$ is the cost proportion of M in year 1 (the other quantities in the equation are similarly defined, also see notation at the end of this book). The expected increase in total unit cost is 4.2 per cent, and this result is obtained both from the DA (deterministic appraisal) and the mean value of the RS (risk simulation) methods. Figures in brackets in Table 8.6 show the standard deviation σ of the simulation results (2.2 in the case of total unit costs). Since well over 99 per cent of outcomes are expected to fall within the range of $\pm 3\sigma$ from the mean, we see from the RS method that the resultant change in total unit cost could be as low as -2 per cent and as high as about 10 per cent. A histogram of the total unit cost, derived from risk simulation, is shown in Fig. 8.2. Similarly, results for changes in the unit cost of materials, wages, capital and other expenses are given in Table 8.6, and histograms may be readily obtained for each of these components.

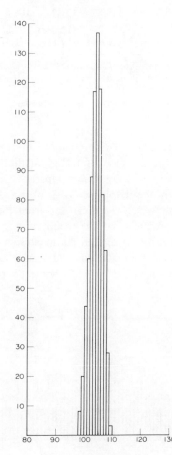

Fig. 8.2. Histogram for total unit costs from risk simulation (768 runs, see p. 142).

In order to estimate the effects of the predicted changes on return on capital, it is necessary to assume selling prices for the slabs produced. For illustrative purposes only the following prices have been selected for the three products:

(1)   Mild steel slabs   £35.00 per ton
(2)   Silicon slabs   £39.34 per ton
(3)   Hire rolled slabs   £3.15 per ton

Table 8.7. Index of Return on Capital and its Determinants

	r	a	e	k
(a) *No price increase*				
DA	72.3	66.4	108.8	100.0
RS–mean	74.4	68.8	107.8	100.0
(st. dev.)	(19.9)	(17.8)	(1.5)	(0)
(b) *Price increase of 5%*				
DA	118.8	109.2	108.8	100.0
RS–mean	120.9	112.0	107.8	100.0
(st. dev.)	(20.4)	(17.8)	(1.5)	(0)

Notes: r = Profit/Total investment
         a = Profit/Output
         e = Output/Capacity
         k = Capacity/Total investment

Again, the DA and the RS were employed to compute the resultant return on investment r, as shown in Table 8.7 and (in the case of risk simulation) in Fig. 8.3. The expected value for return on investment is 74.4 by RS (compared with 100 prior to the changes taking place), which is close to the result of 72.3 obtained by DA, but the range of possible outcomes for r is rather wide, as we can see from Fig. 8.3 and the high standard deviation for r (with a value of 19.9). Of the 1000 runs in the RS method, some 232 runs would have required the plant to exceed its maximum available capacity and were therefore eliminated from the final computations and from the histograms in Figs. 8.2 and 8.3. Of the 768 remaining simulation runs, 674 (or some 88 per cent) resulted in a return

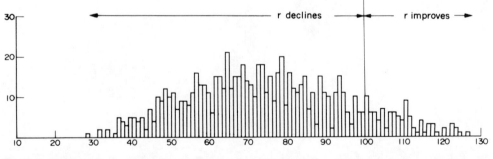

Fig. 8.3. Histogram for return on investment (r) from risk simulation (768 runs) for no price increases.

r below 100. It is also interesting to note the wide spread of the distribution of r in Fig. 8.3, compared with the relatively compact distribution of unit cost in Fig. 8.2.

The change in the expected determinants of the rate of return may also be computed in the same way. We recall from Chapter 7 that $r = aek$; assuming no change in capital investment, the factor k (= capacity/total investment) remains unchanged at 100. The results for a (= unit profit) and e (= capacity utilization) for the DA and RS methods are summarized in Table 8.7, from which it is clear that the major contributor to the reduction in r is the reduction in unit profit, the effect of which is only marginally offset by an expected improvement in utilization.

Turning to the second objective of the analysis—to enable the manager to determine that level of prices for slab output which would ensure that the probability of a fall in the return on capital is no more than, say, 16.6 per cent—it is clear that such questions are not appropriate for the DA method, which is solely concerned with single point estimates. The RS computational procedure allows the distribution of return on investment to be derived, so that the probability of outcomes below or above a given value may be readily obtained. Thus, the RS model may be run for several alternative values of price increases for the output, and we find that for a 5 per cent price increase (for each of the three products in question) the distribution of return on investment in Fig. 8.3 is shifted to the right to a sufficient extent to give the desired result: of 768 simulation runs 644 (or 83.8 per cent) yield a return index of 100 or greater, leaving 16.2 per cent of the outcomes below 100 (note that the expected value of r in this case rises to 120.9, compared with a DA result of 118.8, see Table 8.7). From the RS analysis we therefore conclude that a 5 per cent price increase for the three products will lead to a chance of about 5:1 that the return on investment will not fall below the 100 mark.

The analyses described in this chapter show how the productivity model—coupled with sensitivity tables, deterministic appraisals and/or risk simulation—provide the manager with effective tools to predict likely outcomes. Thus, in addition to the diagnostic nature of the model in examining past behaviour, as described in the case studies in Chapters 4-6, it can be used for control and planning purposes, by allowing the manager to anticipate changes in modes of performance and to take action accordingly.

Reference

1. Eilon, S. and Fowkes, T. R. (eds.) (1972) *Applications of Management Science in Banking and Finance* (chapter 4). Gower Press. London; see also: Sampling procedures for risk simulation. *Operational Research Quarterly*, vol. 24 (1973) no. 2, pp. 242-52.

CHAPTER 9

Conclusions

SAMUEL EILON and JUDITH SOESAN

Empirical studies of industrial operations are usually carried out with one or more of three possible objectives in mind, which characterize the studies as (a) descriptive, (b) predictive and (c) normative.

The purpose of descriptive studies is to establish the pattern of past and current behaviour of a given system and to determine the causal relationships between the major identifiable parameters and components in it. By tracing the pattern of events over a period of time and by recording the level of various performance criteria, the analyst or the manager attempts to construct a model to link these criteria with controllable and uncontrollable variables in the system, so that conclusions can be drawn about the effectiveness or otherwise of past managerial decisions. It is on the basis of an adequate understanding of past behaviour that the analyst can then attempt to make predictions about the future and about the possible consequences of certain alternative actions that may be taken. In making such inferences about future developments and the response of the system to management decisions, the analyst may then wish to assume a normative role and make explicit proposals as to what future actions would be advisable in certain situations.

The measurement and analysis of productivity is a proper field for empirical investigation, and its descriptive role is demonstrated in the case studies in Chapters 4-6 and by the discussion in Chapter 7, while the predictive role of the productivity model is explored in Chapter 8. In the context of managerial control of an enterprise, productivity analysis allows measures of performance to be ascertained, cost and profitability models to be constructed, and an evaluation of past or future operations to be made. This control process, which is schematically described in Fig. 9.1, is based on monitoring current operations, on feedback, and on corrective action; measures of performance are vital if a coherent control process is to be established, and many measures may have to be determined: technological, financial, organizational, procedural and operational. These are not mutually exclusive categories; for example, many financial ratios are imbedded in the measures of productivity discussed throughout this book, as is the evaluation of the effect of technological change, and it is essential to ensure that the various measures are suitably coordinated for multifarious control purposes.

The inter-relationships between the major cost components and their effect on the total cost and profitability structure in an enterprise are demonstrated in Figs. 2.3 and 2.5. They highlight the fact that any single change in the mode of operation reverberates

144

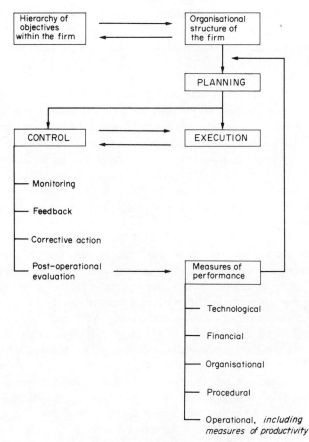

Fig. 9.1. Use of productivity measures.

through the system, **causing** changes to other parameters, including the cost and profit-ability components. Analysis of past data allows discernible trends to be determined, so that their possible future effect on total unit costs and on return on investment may then be evaluated. We have also seen in Chapter 8 how measures of sensitivity can be established and how predictions of future performance can be undertaken, either through a deterministic appraisal, or by a risk simulation approach.

A fundamental issue in any productivity analysis is that of measurement: how to measure multi-inputs and multi-outputs, and how to determine plant capacity and utiliza-tion in a multi-product system which involves sequential processing. The five case studies described in Chapters 4-6 suggest that, within given accounting conventions, the problems of measurement can be overcome. Admittedly, an analyst arriving fresh on an industrial scene will face difficulties in interpreting the records and extracting the information needed for the productivity model; he may find various inconsistencies, changes in accounting procedures, definitions which are incompatible with his needs, varying time lags associated with the information, even gaps in the records. But with the aid of people familiar with the system, and by resorting to reasonable assumptions regarding missing information, the task of constructing the model and the data-bank required for it can be completed without undue difficulty. Needless to say, an enterprise which intends to use the productivity model on a regular basis can so design the monitoring process as to ensure that the relevant data are recorded in a way that is immediately amenable for analysis by the model. The experience we have had with the case studies described in this book suggests that the design of such an information system is not an onerous task and that existing systems with suitable modifications can often serve the purpose.

As we have seen, the model can be used at different levels of aggregation: for the analysis of productivity of a whole industry, or sections of it, for whole plants, for departments, or even with respect to individual processes; comparative studies at different levels can also usefully employ the model: to compare costs and profitability of industries in various countries, to conduct inter-firm comparisons, or to compare the performance of divisions and departments within a given enterprise. This versatility allows the level of disaggregation to be adjusted as a particular study proceeds to meet the operational needs of the entity under scrutiny.

But apart from the level of aggregation from the operational viewpoint, there is the question of aggregation of the data in a given study. Any defined input is capable of disaggregation: labour, for example, can be divided into skilled and unskilled (or into numerous grades), into production and maintenance workers, into normal time and overtime; similarly, materials can be divided into a host of inputs. Such subdivisions make the task of data collection and analysis increasingly difficult (and costly),* particularly when the raw records are not readily presented in sufficient detail. But when certain inputs are subject to possible substitutions and the mix of inputs changes over time, it may not be possible to establish the causes for changes in plant performance without reference to these changes in the input mix. Similarly, the defined product mix may assume different levels of disaggregation: from a completely undifferentiated output, to broad product groups, to sub-groups, to a myriad single products. The problem was well illustrated in the case of steel products in Chapters 5 and 6.

Superimposed on the level of disaggregation of input and output data is the problem of the measurement unit: should, for example, physical labour input be measured in terms of total hours worked or through a weighted measure of disaggregated labour types? The former may be convenient when undifferentiated labour is considered, but when several labour inputs have to be accounted for, then the reduction of the different types (in terms of grade and overtime) to a single common denominator can only be done through a price mechanism.

We have seen some of the problems associated with the measurement of capacity in a capital intensive plant, particularly when processing patterns are complex, when sequential processes are not in balance and when semi-finished products are available for sale. In contrast, the measurement of capacity in a labour-dominated industry is of little consequence, as is that of plant utilization. Similarly, the measurement of fixed capital needs to be conducted against the background of accounting conventions, regarding depreciation procedures and the degree to which inflation and replacement costs should be taken into consideration.

Measurement is, therefore, at the heart of empirical productivity studies. The measurement process gives expression to a given set of definitions and assumptions about the various parameters that make up the production system. It is important to make these assumptions explicit throughout and to appreciate their consequences on the results of calculations from the productivity model and on the interpretations that may be put on these results. In any comparative study, whether it is related to a particular operation over a period of time, or whether it attempts to show how a given plant performs in comparison with another, it is well to remember that the analysis would be valid only for a given set of assumptions regarding definitions and measurement, and provided that consistency is maintained in the manner in which the monitoring process is carried out.

We have highlighted the distinction between the descriptive and the predictive roles of the model, and emphasized that the latter cannot be undertaken without the former. Another distinction often of interest to management is that between the planning and the control functions. The former is concerned with long-term effects, the latter with short-term managerial reaction to current events. A post-operational evaluation (see Fig. 9.1) is essential for planning future activities of an enterprise, and in particular the effect on productivity of such factors as

economies of scale: the extent to which they exist or are likely to develop, based on a comparative study of similar operations conducted at various scales;

working methods: the extent to which changes in operating procedures, manning and organizational structure can influence the performance of a given plant;

new plant: the possible improvement to be gained by replacing plant and machinery, using existing or modified operating procedures;

technological innovation: the expected contribution to be gained from new processes and the way they can be integrated in the plant;

product mix: the likely advantages to be derived from changing the mix, from simplification of the product range, or from its diversification.

Each of these changes (and others not listed here) has financial, technical, marketing, personnel and organizational implications. Each may affect the arrays of inputs and outputs, the unit cost structure, and the profitability of the enterprise. These are central issues in the planning process, and an analysis of the productivity components along the lines described in this book can greatly assist the planners in their task.

But the very same ingredients of the productivity model can be valuable for the control function as well. If appropriate data are monitored on, say, a monthly basis, the model—suitably computerized—can be used to produce monthly reports on changes in the cost structure, and (with the methods described in Chapter 8) to produce up-dated sensitivity tables, deterministic appraisals based on established trends, or even risk simulations run automatically on certain assumptions. With a remote terminal, it is not difficult to run the model in a "conversational mode", with the manager directing the deterministic appraisals and the risk simulations to be re-run with fresh sets of assumptions, if needed, so that on the basis of the results (which can be obtained within minutes) he can then decide what adjustments it would be advisable to make in the short term in the operating conditions of the plant.

The productivity model was originally developed for manufacturing industry, and its application at the plant level is ostensibly demonstrated by the case studies described in this book. There is no reason, however, why similar concepts could not be employed in the analysis of productivity in various service industries, where interest in productivity and its measurement is steadily mounting. Take as an example supermarkets and department stores: although no conversion of "raw materials" into "products" takes place in the manufacturing sense of the term, we can easily identify arrays of inputs and outputs with

147

their corresponding costs and prices. "Plant capacity" may perhaps be measured by the available usable space and its utilization may be a function of the throughput channelled through the given space during a specified time interval.

A somewhat more complicated operation is one where some of the inputs and most of the outputs are not physical entities. A clearing bank, for example, consists of a network of branches, which provide a variety of services to its customers. Ignoring for a moment the activities at head-office and the many specialized non-domestic banking operations, we are left with the retail network, in which each branch is a well-defined entity with reasonably well-defined tasks. Inputs (other than labour, stationery and other expenses), outputs, capacity and utilization are more difficult to measure than in a manufacturing environment, and the profit contribution of a bank branch is perhaps less tangible than that of a manufacturing unit. In principle, however, it should be possible to construct a model, akin to that described in this book, for the purpose of analysing productivity components in non-manufacturing operations.

Productivity analysis is not a panacea to solve all managerial problems, but it has the attribute of great flexibility, and with suitable modifications the basic model described in this book can be adapted for use in a wide variety of situations. Properly applied, it can become an indispensable tool to aid management to understand the intricate performance behaviour of industrial enterprises and to provide invaluable information for the planning and control of operations.

Appendix

MAIN NOTATION

δ	increment, e.g. δa is increment of a
a	$p - c$ = unit profit for the output
a^*	relative change of $a = \delta a / a$
c	unit cost for the output
e	capacity utilization
e^*	relative change of $e = \delta e / e$
k	capacity/total investment
k^*	relative change of $k = \delta k / k$
p	unit price for the output
r	return on total investment
r^*	relative change of $r = \delta r / r$

AUI_F	actively utilized fixed investment
C	capital
CAP	capacity
CC	capital charges or depreciation charges
DA	deterministic appraisal
I_F	fixed investment
I_T	total investment
M	materials
M-hr	man-hours
M_V	materials volume
OE	other expenses
$P(A)$	price for product A
$P_n(A)$	price for product A in year n
PO	output
$(PO)_{n,1}$	ratio of output in year n to output in year 1
RS	risk simulation
$Q_n(A)$	quantity of product A in year n
TC	total unit cost
V_n	value of output in year n
W	wages
Z	profit

149

Index